Dorchester

St. Mary's Infant Asylum and Maternity Hospital was opened in 1882 in the Green
Mansion at the crest of Cushing Avenue near Upham's Corner, Dorchester. The Sisters of
Charity of St. Vincent de Paul operated it as a "house of reception for unwanted babies."
By the mid-twentieth century, St. Margaret's Hospital, as it later became known, was the
largest maternity hospital in Boston.

Dorchester
A COMPENDIUM

Anthony Mitchell Sammarco

Charleston   London

THE
History
PRESS

Published by The History Press
Charleston, SC 29403
www.historypress.net

First published 2011

Manufactured in the United States

ISBN 978.1.60949.217.5

Library of Congress Cataloging-in-Publication Data

Sammarco, Anthony Mitchell.
Dorchester : a compendium / Anthony Mitchell Sammarco.
p. cm.
Summary: A collection of articles that first appeared in the Dorchester community notes.
ISBN 978-1-60949-217-5
1. Dorchester (Boston, Mass.)--History. 2. Dorchester (Boston, Mass.)--Social life and
customs. 3. Dorchester (Boston, Mass.)--Biography. 4. Boston (Mass.)--History. 5. Boston
(Mass.)--Social life and customs. 6. Boston (Mass.)--Biography. I. Dorchester community
notes. II. Title.
F74.D5S265 2011
974.4'61--dc22
2011004505

In Memory of Paul G. Buchanan

CONTENTS

ACKNOWLEDGEMENTS

*D*orchester: A Compendium is a selection of articles that appeared in the *Dorchester Community News* from 1982 to 2002. During that two-decades-long association, I was honored, in 1987, to be named Dorchester Town Historian in a proclamation from city of Boston mayor Raymond L. Flynn and to have received the Bulfinch Award from the Doric Dames of the Massachusetts State House and the George Washington Medal from the Freedom Foundation. I was encouraged by editors Mark Pickering, Margaret Lamb, Sean Cahill and Peter Van Delft to research and write these articles on the fascinating history, architecture and development of this very special neighborhood of the city of Boston.

I would like to thank the following people and organizations for their assistance, kindness, encouragement and support over the many years of researching the rich and ever-evolving history of Dorchester: the Animal Rescue League; the late Janet Bergeron; the late Sally Clemens Birch; Anthony Bognanno; Priscilla Hall Bone; the Boston Athenaeum, Catharina Slautterback and Patricia Boulos; Helen G. Buchanan; Mary Jo Campbell; Joe Cedrone; Frank Cheney; Elise Ciregna and Stephen Lo Piccolo; Elizabeth and Mary Clapp; Edith Clifford; Regina Clifton; Joseph Costa; Elizabeth Curtiss; Doric Dames of the Massachusetts State House; Marion Diener; William Dillon; Olivia Grant Dybing; the late Dr. Lydia Bowman Edwards; Frances Pierce Field; First Parish Church, Dorchester, and Reverend Arthur Lavoie; Catherine Flannery; Julia and John B. Fox; the late Walter S. Fox; the Freedom Foundation; Dale H. Freeman, digital resource archivist, University of Massachusetts; the late Ardelle Moseley Fullerton; Philip Gavin; Stephen Wentworth Gifford; Jean Goldman and Vincent Da Forno; Edward W. Gordon; the late Roger Greene; Joan Halpert and Peter Hanson; Helen Hannon; Dorothy Johnson Henry; James Hobin; Jon Hogan and Gaveston Nguyen; the late Virginia Holbrook; the late Elizabeth B. Hough; the late Veronica Lehane; Jane Lindsay; Phil Lindsay; Paul Leo and David McGinniss; Judith McGillicuddy; Karen Mac Nutt, Esq.; Martin Manning; John Franklin May; the late Dagmar Pierce Merna; Elizabeth Mock, retired archivist, University of Massachusetts; the late Curtis Norris; Frank Norton; Susan W. Paine; William H. Pear II; Loretta Philbrick; Scott Piatov; Daniel Pierce; the late Roger Pierce; Lilian M.C. Randall; the late Ruth Raycraft; Mary Cifrino Roever; Jeffrey Saraceno, my editor; Robert Bayard Severy; the Shelburne Museum and Jean Burks; Letitia Carruth Stone; the late Martha R. Sullivan; Jane Taylor; William O. Taylor II; the late William Vandervoort Tripp; the Urban College of Boston; the Victorian Society, New England Chapter; Steven Walker, South End Photo Lab; the late Dorothy C. Wallace; Ann and Tom Walsh; Ellen and Tom White; Virginia M. White; the Winterthur Library and Jeanne Solensky; and the late Marion W. Woodbridge.

Unless otherwise noted, all photographs are from the Sammarco Collection, Archives and Special Collections, Joseph P. Healey Library, University of Massachusetts at Boston, which a portion of the royalties from this book will benefit.

1

TOWN OF DORCHESTER

DORCHESTER TOWN SEAL

In 1865, the selectmen of Dorchester appointed a committee of three to "procure a seal, with suitable device, as a Corporate Seal of the town of Dorchester." The committee consisted of Edmund J. Baker, Edmund Pitt Tileston and Nathaniel W. Tileston, leading citizens of the town and all shareholders in two of the more important mills on the Neponset River, the Walter Baker Chocolate Company and the Tileston & Hollingsworth Paper Company.

The town of Dorchester was founded in June 1630 by a group of Puritans who had gathered at the New Hospital in Plymouth, England, prior to their departure for the New World. It was there that they founded their church, carrying its charter to their eventual settlement in Massachusetts Bay Colony. In the Dorchester Town Seal, the rudimentary aspects of the early settlement were expressed in the "thatch-roofed church which appears, without a chimney" at its center. Since Dorchester had the first free public school in the country, the committee included that "humble, thatched-roof building in the lower part of the shield, a little to the rear of the church." The early industrial growth of the town was depicted by the inclusion of Israel Stoughton's gristmill, founded in 1634 on the Neponset River. The "rude mill, with its large wheel, which is set upon the left bank of the Neponset River, the course of [which] from its source to its mouth, lay through the ancient territory of Dorchester."

The Dorchester
Town Seal was
designed in 1865 by
Edmund J. Baker,
Edmund Pitt Tileston
and Nathaniel W.
Tileston, who were
charged by the
town selectmen to
"procure a seal, with
suitable device, as a
Corporate Seal of the
town of Dorchester."

With true concern about the important aspects of the early settlement of the town, the committee included in the motto of the seal "*Pietate, Literis, Industria*" signifying that piety, learning and industry were among the prominent virtues of the Puritans who settled Dorchester and were shared by their descendants. The seal also includes the Great Blue Hills to the rear of the church, school and mill, signifying the extent of the settlement and the hills' prominent reference in the early writings of the selectmen. In deference to the town from which many of the Puritans came, the top of the shield features a triple-towered castle with battlements. This was included as a sign of reverence for England and the fact that the Puritans left their home to establish a settlement that allowed freedom of religion.

The Neponset River, named after the Massachusetts tribe of Native Americans that inhabited the area for centuries, flows through the center of the seal and further links itself to Stoughton's gristmill. The Blue Hills in the background recall that Dorchester once included lands far to the south. In the seventeenth century, Dorchester comprised the following towns: South Boston, Hyde Park, Milton, Squantum, Canton, Foxboro, Wrentham, Raynham and Stoughton. The land extended far beyond the Blue Hills and brought the boundary close to that of Rhode Island. In 1865, the town of

The Dorchester Town Hall was built in 1816 at Baker's Corner, now known as Codman Square. The separation of church and state necessitated a town hall, built at the corner of Washington and Norfolk Streets, which was used until the annexation of the town to Boston in 1870.

Dorchester had recently participated in the Civil War, and patriotism was running high. The committee, composed of three of the leading citizens of the day, created a well-planned and appropriate device that remains the seal of a town that now only exists as a neighborhood of the city of Boston. Dorchester was annexed by Boston on January 4, 1870.

FIREWARD SOCIETY OF DORCHESTER AND MILTON

It's somewhat difficult to imagine a community without a fire department, for the prevention and battling of fires is of the utmost importance. However, the first fire department in Dorchester and Milton was not established until after the Revolutionary War. The Fireward Society of Dorchester and Milton was established in 1793 with individuals from both towns assisting in the purchase of a fire engine to protect the property of share owners. The Fireward Society had one hundred shareholders who subscribed not only to purchase the fire engine but also to maintain the engine in a small building that was located on the Dorchester side of the bridge spanning the Neponset River at the Lower Mills.

The committee of the Fireward Society, and the clerk, Stephen Badlam, issued shares to subscribers for "the relief of those who may be distressed with calamitous Fire." The method of battling a fire at this time was to have a group of volunteers form in a line between the engine and the nearest source of water, passing fire buckets from hand to hand until they were emptied into the tub of the fire engine. Once enough water had been dumped into the tub of the engine, the volunteers would then squirt the water at the fire by means of a hand pump. After the assembling of the volunteers, the filling of the leather fire buckets and the squirting of the water had taken place, one wonders how many burning buildings were actually saved two centuries ago.

The first fire engine was known as Fountain Engine Number 1 and was owned by the shareholders of both Dorchester and Milton. The fire engine, operated by a hand pump, was manned by volunteers from both towns. Their service, though voluntary, was remunerated by their exemption from military duty and by the refunding of their poll tax by the towns. Thirty-two men from the towns of Dorchester and Milton made a large enough pool of volunteers, and their authority was strictly limited to the scene of a fire,

Fountain Engine No. 1 was the hand-pump engine of the Fireward Society of Dorchester and Milton, founded in 1793. A shareholding society, subscribers paid for their share, and services were rendered for "the relief of those who may be distressed with calamitous fire."

where their mission of firefighting and their obedience to orders had to be observed, with penalties for refusal to obey. Their duties, strictly volunteer, were to attend all fires and to assist in both the fighting of the fire and the direction of assistance at the fire. Their uniforms were haphazard, but each volunteer was provided with a leather helmet emblazoned with "Fireward Society in Dorchester and Milton, Fountain No. 1" in bold letters.

Two centuries ago, the Lower Mills, known as Neponset Village until 1832, was the site of most industrial concerns for both Dorchester and Milton. The first chocolate mills in this country (Baker, Preston, Webb & Twombley and Dr. Ware's Chocolate) were located along the Neponset River, as were paper mills, gristmills and a playing card factory. The Lower Mills had numerous cabinetmakers, among them Stephen Badlam and Edward H.R. Ruggles, two prominent residents. The shop of Benjamin Crehore, who produced the first American bass viol, pianoforte and artificial leg in this country, had his shop on the Milton side of the river, so it is not surprising that the shareholders of the Fireward Society opted to house their new fire engine in the Lower Mills, where most of the shareholders' homes and mills were located.

The Fireward Society, though a necessary and vitally important service to both towns, was primarily a social and fraternal group of men who often had musters and participated in parades. Their competitions, whereby they filled their engine with water and tried to shoot the water from the hand pump higher than a competitor's, made for both an enjoyable competition and community pride were they to win. The thrill and excitement of a group of volunteers engaged in this sport led to a good-natured rivalry. Edward Pierce Hamilton, author of *A History of Milton*, said:

> *If one thinks of a fire company of this period as being essentially a social organization with some fire-fighting obligations as a side issue, he would not be far from wrong. Even today with all our competing thrills and spectacles, a fire has tremendous appeal to all. In those more placid days, the opportunity to belong to a congenial group of friends with a clubhouse provided free, and the ever-present hope of a good lively fire to dash to and perhaps to try to fight, presented a great appeal to many a man.*

As we reflect on the founding over two centuries ago of the Fireward Society of Dorchester and Milton, we can look back with pride on the determination of our ancestors to establish so necessary an organization. Today we salute the Boston Fire Department and the Milton Fire Department, for though our taxes now support fire engines and the departments, we are indebted to our towns' earliest efforts to aid "those who may be distressed with calamitous fire."

LYCEUM HALL

Lyceum Hall used to stand across from the First Parish Church on Meeting House Hill. The puddingstone ledge there provided a firm foundation for a hall that aimed to carry on the traditions of the philosopher Aristotle. Of course, the first lyceum, a public lecture hall, was in ancient Greece. However, the ideals of democracy, which first took root in that country, had a vast impact on many aspects of early nineteenth-century Boston culture.

In 1839, Dorchester residents voted to erect a lecture hall on town land on Meeting House Hill. The town selectmen then appointed a building committee, which was chaired by Colonel Walter Baker, the wealthy owner of the Baker Chocolate Company at the Dorchester Lower Mills. The committee also included Samuel Loud, John Robinson, Thomas Tremlett, William Draper Swan, Moses Draper and Oliver Hall. The committee's job was to raise the necessary funds to build a hall, and it appealed to its fellow townsmen with a pamphlet entitled *Address to Our Fellow Citizens*, which argued that the hall would be a benefit to the town. It would, the committee said, provide a place for public discussion and debate on subjects of common interest. The Lyceum Hall would also provide another public space that could be used for a multitude of purposes. The town hall, located at Baker's Corner (now Codman Square) and in use from 1816, was a good walk from Meeting House Hill. A new lyceum would be convenient for residents in the northern part of town.

On February 27, 1840, Lyceum Hall was officially dedicated. The famous educator Horace Mann spoke, while Colonel Baker presided. With great ceremony, the Lyceum Hall was accepted by the selectmen of Dorchester from the building committee, and a hymn composed by the Reverend John Pierpont for the occasion was sung. In all, the dedication was one of the finest seen in Dorchester and attracted attention far and wide. Lyceum Hall was built in the then-fashionable Greek Revival style, with a stately portico

Lyceum Hall was built just south of the First Parish Church in Dorchester and dedicated in February 1840. This 1847 lithograph by Lemuel Blackman depicts the 1816 church designed by Oliver Warren at Meeting House Hill, with Lyceum Hall on the right and the common in the foreground. *Courtesy of the Boston Athenaeum.*

with four Ionic columns gracing the façade. The hall, a large gallery, and two anterooms came to serve the diverse needs of a growing population. Baker had made extremely generous donations to the building fund, and the committee wished to dedicate the hall to him. He declined the honor, and the name Lyceum Hall became official.

Throughout the nineteenth century, the hall was the site of educational lectures, demonstrations, dances and military drills. The hall served as the recruiting station for the Civil War, and work tables were set up for women who cut cloth bandages for the army. The first Episcopal mass in Dorchester (1847), the first Roman Catholic Mass on Meeting House Hill (1872) and the Free Society, a Unitarian church (1881–82) were held here. The hall showed no bias and served as a steady and prominent building on the hill. In the 1860s, the First Parish Church began using the hall for choir rehearsals and for its Sunday school classes. However, after the annexation of Dorchester to the city of Boston in 1870, the use of Lyceum Hall began to change. It was still used for dances, socials and concerts, but during the day it was used by local schools for mechanical arts, woodworking and sundry purposes that served the growing population. By the Great Depression, the First Parish Church was one of the few community groups still using the stately hall. The City of Boston School Department used the space for mentally challenged students, in addition to the shop classes still being conducted there. But no longer was the lecture by a visiting Harvard professor or a dance with the Germania Band a large enough drawing card to the Lyceum Hall, as movie houses, along with the Strand Theatre and attractions in Boston, drew residents away.

After an unsuccessful attempt by local residents to save the building, primarily led by the First Parish Church, Lyceum Hall was demolished in 1955. The relatively new Sturbridge Village had declined to accept Lyceum Hall, saying that it was not a significant enough building. No further use for it could be found by the city after the school department stopped holding classes there. Today, we look back at a time when the Lyceum Hall provided not only an educational service but also a meeting place for our ancestors.

EDWARD EVERETT SQUARE

Five Corners in Dorchester is the junction of Boston, East Cottage and West Cottage Streets, Columbia Road and Massachusetts Avenue. The earliest intersection in town, it dates to the seventeenth century, but in the ensuing three centuries it has collected many more angles than five corners. Known today as Edward Everett Square, the intersection just east of Upham's Corner is a major traffic connector to Roxbury and the South End, the Southeast Expressway and Andrew Square in South Boston.

Named for the great statesman, orator and native-born son whose bronze statue designed in 1866 by William Wetmore Story stands with uplifted hand in Richardson Park, Edward Everett (1794–1865) was born in a house that originally stood on the site of Dunkin' Donuts. Of course, it was rural at that time, but it's a bit of trivia that you might contemplate the next time you are in line for a cup of coffee. Columbia Road was laid out with streetcar tracks that extended from South Boston to Roxbury; originally known as Boston Street (a continuation of the present street by that name), it eventually became known as Columbia Street just west of Upham's Corner to Blue Hill Avenue. In 1893, the two streets were regraded, straightened

Edward Everett (1794–1865) was born in the mansion built in 1746 by the Oliver family at Five Corners, subsequently known as Edward Everett Square. Everett was later to serve as president of Harvard College, ambassador to the court of Saint James and as the foremost orator of the nineteenth century.

and renamed Columbia Road and became part of the Emerald Necklace begun by Frederick Law Olmsted. His successors, the Olmsted Associates, created a green space extending from Franklin Park to Marine Park in South Boston that ran along the center of Columbia Road. Though the trees no longer survive along the center green strip today, it must have been attractive with the automobile road on either side of the streetcar tracks in the center.

By the early twentieth century, Dorchester's contribution to American architecture was being built with alacrity. The three-decker, a wood-framed building with three independent apartments in a vertical rise, had its start in Dorchester in the late 1880s and would eventually represent over 30 percent of the housing stock of the town. Looking in either direction along Columbia Road, three-deckers were built between one-family houses and large apartment buildings. Three-deckers created an impressive streetscape

Looking east on Columbia Road toward Edward Everett Square in 1929, the once rural crossroads known as Five Corners had been built up with three-deckers, creating a distinctly urban neighborhood. The bronze statue of Edward Everett (1794–1865) can be seen in the center of the circular park.

when they were built in multiple units, sharing a uniformity of rooflines, similar projections and similar building materials and designs. Three-deckers in Dorchester were, quite literally, the red brick row houses of Boston's South End or the brownstone town houses of Boston's Back Bay. With front and rear porches, Colonial Revival detailing, interior plumbing and fixtures and the circulation of air on all four sides, three-deckers were a godsend to those who sought home ownership with the added benefit of rental income from the apartments to assist in paying the mortgage.

Though some of the three-deckers along Columbia Road survive, some have been razed and replaced with infill housing, such as the Edward Everett Square Town Houses, red brick, two-story apartments built in 2000 at the corner of Columbia Road and West Cottage Street.

CODMAN SQUARE

Codman Square was named in 1848 in memory of the Reverend John Codman (1782–1847), the late pastor of the Second Church in Dorchester. Codman was a well-respected leader of the town who had served the church since 1807. Previously, the area had been known as Baker's Corner in honor of Dr. James Baker, who kept a dry goods store at the corner of Talbot Avenue and Washington Street (the present site of the Lithgow Building). Baker graduated from Harvard College in 1760 and began his career teaching school in Dorchester. Obviously this position did not suit him, for he was keeping his store by 1765. That same year, he met John Hannon, who was to help Baker found the first chocolate mill on the Neponset River.

Baker's Corner at the time of the Revolution was sparsely settled, with large tracts of farmland owned by the Davenport, Capen and Baker families. The area remained virtually undeveloped until the split occurred in Dorchester's First Parish Church. Officially, it was stated that the increase in the town's population necessitated having another place of worship; however, differences over religious doctrine were at the root of the split. The

The Second Congregational Church was built in 1805 at the corner of Washington and Centre Streets. An impressive and elegant meetinghouse, the four-sided clock was donated by Walter Baker, and the church boasted a bell cast by Paul Revere & Son.

congregation of the Second Church, composed of former members of the First Parish Church, built its meetinghouse in 1805 in Baker's Corner, then still a relatively obscure area of Dorchester. The Second Church embraced the more traditional beliefs of orthodox Congregationalism, as opposed to the more liberal Unitarian belief that prevailed at First Parish Church. The split, amicable at first, later led to a fierce rivalry that lasted many decades.

The Second Church commanded an important position in the square. Centre Street was an old Indian pathway that led to Norfolk Street, the old road to Dedham. Washington Street (known as the Upper Road) was the road that led, as directly as possible, from Boston to Milton and beyond. The crossroads began to take on new importance when, in 1816, the Town of Dorchester voted to separate church and state and build a town hall in Baker's Corner.

The area was considered Dorchester Centre, as it is still known by the postal marks today. Because of its central location, the area was chosen as the site for the new town hall. Until this was built, town meetings were held at the churches. The town hall was to serve the needs of the growing

The Clap-Kendall House was on Washington Street, between Kenwood and Moultrie Streets. On the far left can be seen the Dorchester Academy at the corner of Lyndhurst Street.

community admirably from 1816 until 1870, the year Dorchester was annexed to Boston. But Dorchester's needs were changing, and the town hall became superfluous. It was demolished and replaced by the Codman Square Branch of the Boston Public Library, now the Great Hall of the Codman Square Health Center. The Dorchester High School was built in the 1890s on the eastern side of the square, with the prestigious firm of Hartwell & Richardson designing the Classical Revival school of yellow brick. The school later became Dorchester High School for Girls and later Girls' Latin School before being remodeled for apartments in the 1980s. The Dorchester Woman's Club, founded in 1892, built its impressive clubhouse, designed by local architect A. Warren Gould, on Centre Street.

Overall, Codman Square changed dramatically after the Civil War. The Clap-Kendall estate was subdivided in the 1890s for Moultrie, Kenwood and Lyndhurst Streets and Melville Avenue. The Kendalls retained their Federal house, built in 1796, which stood on the site of the People's Market on Washington Street. The Means family, of the Second Church, had the house next door. The historic Capen House, thought to have been built in

The Torrey Mansion was designed by Cabot & Chandler and built in 1886 for Elbridge Torrey (1837–1914) at the corner of Washington Street and Melville Avenue. In the last half of the nineteenth century, many architect-designed houses were built in the fashionable "streetcar suburb" of Dorchester.

1636, was just down the street, across from Melville Avenue, and was moved to Milton in 1919. Developers began to create an attractive "streetcar suburb," the growth of which was fueled by the convenience of the Old Colony Railroad, which had stations at Field's Corner and Shawmut. With the railroad offering a convenient commute to Boston, the rapid building of Jewell Park commenced. Waldeck Street, a curving cross street, was laid out with cross streets running from east to west. Lindsey, Larchmont and Tonawanda Streets were all cut through the old Roswell Gleason estate. Similarly, the old Walter Baker estate, which adjoined that of Gleason, was subdivided. Roswell Gleason was the first person to silver plate metal in this country, and his successful factory for Britannia ware, similar to pewter, was located at what is now Mother's Rest Park. The Bakers, who owned the Baker Chocolate Company at the Lower Mills, had adapted as their home the old Oliver Mansion, which was built prior to the Revolution. The subdivision of these two estates created numerous building lots for both upper-middle-class and middle-class houses. By 1900, the neighborhood was entirely built up. Making comparisons between what the area looked like in 1900 versus 1800 would be almost fruitless, as Codman Square had few landmarks in the early nineteenth century other than the Second Church and the town hall.

The turn-of-the-twentieth-century shopping area in Codman Square, or Dorchester Centre, was superior, with the Kennedy Butter & Egg Company, W.T. Grant's Store, the Dorchester Savings Bank and Schiff's Pharmacy. The attractiveness of the arching trees of the Second Church lawn and the stately elms that lined Washington Street made the walk to the square a pleasure.

PORT NORFOLK

Port Norfolk is today separated from the rest of Dorchester by the wide swath of the Southeast Expressway. Once adjacent to Neponset, it is today both visually and pedestrian separated from the area, but when it was developed, it was laid out as a planned neighborhood for Dorchester's increasing population. Luther Briggs Jr. (1822–1905) was commissioned by Edward King, president of the Neponset Wharf Company, to survey and lay out new streets in the area formerly known as Pine Neck.

Port Norfolk was laid out by Luther Briggs Jr. (1822–1905). The Second Methodist Episcopal Church (later the Church of the Unity) is in the center, with houses at Wood and Walnut Streets fronting onto the tracks of the Old Colony Railroad. *Courtesy of the Boston Athenaeum.*

Pine Neck, which remained undeveloped for over two centuries after Dorchester was settled in 1630, had a slight knoll in the center that was covered in conifers. The area was renamed Port Norfolk, in relation to the waterfront port and creek and the fact that Dorchester was then part of Norfolk County. Briggs laid out new streets, including Walnut Street, which he graded with 278 loads of gravel and in many instances designed and built new residences. He was an able surveyor, respected architect and the nephew of the noted Boston architect Alexander Parris, with whom he worked as a draftsman from 1839 to 1842. Parris designed Quincy Market at Dock Square, St. Paul's Episcopal Cathedral and numerous other buildings in Boston. Briggs later became associated with Gridley J. Fox Bryant in 1842, an architectural partnership that lasted two years, after which Briggs established an independent architectural practice. Later, building his own residence on Walnut Street in Port Norfolk. He would remain in the neighborhood until his death.

The Greek Revival–style Methodist Episcopal Church in Port Norfolk (later the Church of the Unity) was organized in 1848 and soon flourished with the new residents. Some of the major streets were Walnut Street, Rice Street (originally called Wood Street Court) and Wood (now Woodworth) Street. Remarkably, though the church does not survive, the three houses next to it do and give a major example of how Port Norfolk was envisioned and planned in the mid-nineteenth century. The Dr. Henry Blanchard House

Charles Austin Wood (1818–1898) was a noted local architect who lived at Port Norfolk and designed residences as well as the impressive Second French Empire Dorchester Mutual Fire Insurance Company headquarters on Walnut Street. He also designed his granite Egyptian Revival tomb at the Old North Burying Ground in Dorchester.

at 5 Rice Street is a late Greek Revival house with a cupola surmounting the roof; adjacent is the Isaac Stetson House, which was more Italianate in design with cast-iron rails on its stairs. The third house was the home of Charles Austin Wood, a well-known local architect, and later became the home of the Thomas French Temple. Despite the fact that Luther Briggs Jr. designed all of these houses after Port Norfolk was laid out in 1845, and the fact that they have been changed by their current residents, they remarkably survive.

The Old Colony Railroad, founded in 1844 by Nathan Carruth, connected Kneeland Street in Boston with towns on the South Shore. In the fall of 1845, a commuter station known as the Neponset Station was opened at Port Norfolk, the last stop before the trains crossed the Neponset River via a bridge to Quincy.

ASHMONT

Ashmont is a neighborhood east of Peabody Square. Once the eighteen-acre estate of Nathan Carruth, first president of the Old Colony Railroad, it was eventually subdivided by Herbert Shaw Carruth and became a quintessential streetcar suburb neighborhood of Boston between 1882 and 1917. Herbert Shaw Carruth (1856–1919) inherited much of his father's estate upon his death in 1881; his father's house was originally at the crest of the hill and was known as Beechmont. Carruth and Beaumont Streets were originally the carriage drive to the house, which was eventually demolished in 1911. The Ellen H. Richards School, designed by Dorchester architect William H. Besarick, was built on its site.

In the 1889 edition of the *Dorchester Handbook*, the precursor to the *Dorchester Blue Books*, Herbert Shaw Carruth was said, in a short biography, to deserve

> *much credit for the building up and beautifying of this section of Dorchester. Mr. Carruth's father, the late Nathan Carruth, formerly owned the greater part of the land, which now comprises Ashmont, and the son has, by careful but honorable and square dealings, increased the value of the*

Herbert Shaw Carruth (1855–1917) was said by the *Dorchester Beacon* to be "honest in purpose, outspoken in opinion, quick in judgment and often hasty in word and action." Nevertheless, he ably developed his father's estate, Beechmont, into one of the more picturesque neighborhoods of Dorchester. Carruth served as an alderman of the city of Boston and was the first executive officer of the Metropolitan Parks Commission.

original property ten-fold. Mr. Carruth has built more than forty houses of handsome architectural design during the last five years.

In the period between 1884 and 1889, not only were new streets laid out as public thoroughfares, but Carruth also developed his father's estate as an impressive, cohesive and upscale residential development that was within walking distance of the Ashmont Station of the Old Colony Railroad. In this period, Carruth either commissioned architects such as John A. Fox, Edwin J. Lewis Jr., Whitney Lewis and Joseph Tilden Greene to design and build speculative houses or sold land to new residents who were required by their deeds to build architect-designed houses.

On Beaumont Street, which was extended in 1877 from Carruth to Adams Streets, were the Smith Nichols House (24 Beaumont Street), designed by John A. Fox, and Herbert Shaw Carruth's own house (30 Beaumont Street), designed by Luther Briggs Jr. On the opposite side of the street are the

The Carruth House was designed by Dorchester architect Luther Briggs Jr. and built at 30 Beaumont Street, the former carriage drive to Beechmont, the estate of his father, Nathan Carruth.

Charles Read and Gideon Abbott Houses (11 and 17 Beaumont Street, respectively) and the palatial Samuel H.L. Pierce House (53 Beaumont Street). These new houses, representing the best in suburban architecture in Dorchester, would later include other houses, such as the Jacques House (30 Carruth Street), designed by Joseph Tilden Greene. Frederick Jacques was partners with George B. Griffin in the 1884 Whitney Lewis–designed grocery store Jacques & Griffin (now O'Brien's Market in Peabody Square).

In the nineteenth century, Dorchester's population swelled from 12,000 in 1870, the year Dorchester was annexed to the city of Boston, to 100,000 three decades later. Herbert Shaw Carruth's development of his father's estate, Beechmont, in Ashmont was testimony to his commitment to what is today considered one of Dorchester's most charming neighborhoods.

PIERCE SQUARE

The Lower Mills is the junction of Dorchester Avenue and Washington and Adams Streets and was, in 1897, named Pierce Square in honor of Henry L. Pierce, president of the Baker Chocolate Company and mayor of Boston in 1872 and 1877. However, the area was also known as "Unquety" by its original inhabitants, the Neponset tribe of Massachusetts Indians. Unquety referred to the lower falls, as opposed to the upper falls, or what they called "Unquetyquisset" (present-day Mattapan). Though these various names all apply to the Lower Mills, the Puritans who settled Dorchester referred to this area as "Neponset" until 1832, when the area that now bears the name, stretching from Pope's Hill to Neponset Circle, was so named. The Lower Mills, though only five miles from Edward Everett Square, which borders Roxbury and South Boston, was the industrial area of Dorchester. The town's first gristmill was erected in 1634, when Israel Stoughton was granted permission to erect a water-powered gristmill. Within a few decades, the Lower Mills had the first gunpowder mill, the first paper mill, the first chocolate mill and the first playing card mill in the United States.

Though Dorchester's population was widespread and never exceeded eight thousand until after the Civil War, the Lower Mills was an area where many people lived in proximity to their place of employment. Not only were the Upper Road (Washington Street) and the Lower Road (Adams Street) streets that led directly to the Lower Mills, but also Dorchester Turnpike

Henry Lillie Pierce (1825–1896) was the president of the Baker Chocolate Company from 1845 to 1896. He served as mayor of Boston in 1872 and 1877 and as a United States congressman from 1873 to 1877.

(now Avenue) was laid out in 1805 to connect the industrial concerns in the Lower Mills with Boston. Dorchester Turnpike was a toll road that one had to pay a fee (per weight if one's cart carried products from the area) to use. As the two other streets that flanked it were "free streets" that one was not required to pay to use, Yankee frugality ruled out and led to the failure of the toll road.

During the 1830 to 1860 period, the "mill village" perception of the Lower Mills began to change as large numbers of millworkers moved to the area in search of employment. These workers, mostly immigrants from western Europe, came from many different religious groups and countries, and they founded numerous churches that diversified the religious mix of Dorchester. By the Civil War, the Congregational and Unitarian faiths were joined by Methodist Episcopalians, Episcopalians, Baptists and Roman Catholics, and the spectrum of European countries represented was even more diverse.

Pierce Square, seen in the distance from Washington Street, was named in January 1897 in memory of Henry L. Pierce. The junction of Dorchester Avenue and Washington and Adams Streets was transformed into an urban crossroads by Pierce, with mills designed by Nathaniel J. Bradlee and his successor firm, Bradlee, Winslow & Wetherall, between 1872 and 1896.

The Lower Mills is a fine example of a mill village, where not only mills survive but also workers' row housing, mill managers' houses and a residential district within a specific area. When the Neponset River was harnessed for water power in the seventeenth century, it spawned an industrial area that had a spectrum of mills, workers and history.

Four Corners

Four Corners is the junction of Washington, Bowdoin and Harvard Streets. Simply named, it is the intersection of four corners, yet the history of this neighborhood is fascinating. Washington Street was originally known as the Upper Road, laid out in 1654. Most of what was surrounding land in the seventeenth and eighteenth centuries was farmland, with Governor James

Washington Street, between Crown Path and Dakota Street, had houses that were owned by Roswell Gleason and rented to his Britannia ware factory workers. In the early twentieth century, this area was cleared for Mother's Rest, a park with a breathtaking panoramic view of Dorchester Bay and Boston Harbor.

Bowdoin's summerhouse surmounting Mount Bowdoin; the area remained largely undeveloped until after the Civil War. Four Corners was a crossroads, with Harvard Street leading to the Brush Hill Turnpike (Blue Hill Avenue), which was laid out as a toll road connecting Roxbury and Milton in 1805. Washington Street was laid out to connect Roxbury at Grove Hall to the Lower Mills, and Bowdoin Street connected Four Corners to Kane Square just below Meeting House Hill.

However, after the Revolution, the area around Four Corners was a prime location, as the view from the Upper Road toward the harbor was unparalleled. This panoramic view, seen from Boston all the way to Squantum, was a reason to build houses along the road. One of the first houses belonged to Edmund Pitt Tileston, a partner in the firm of Tileston & Hollingsworth, a paper mill on the Neponset River. He had a large Federal mansion at the corner of Washington and Dakota Streets that had a splendid view. The well-manicured grounds included terraces and a goldfish pond on the present site of Claybourne Street. Adjacent to this estate was a small cottage that was once the home of Edwin and Mary Devlin Booth. He was a noted Shakespearean actor and brother of the notorious John Wilkes Booth, assassin of President Abraham Lincoln. The Booths had moved to Dorchester from Boston for the "healthy air," as Mrs. Booth suffered from consumption. In Booth's biography, *The Prince of Players*, it is said that the Booths moved to Dorchester to be near Dr. Erasmus Miller, a noted consumptive doctor who lived at the corner of Washington and School Streets.

The commercial development of Four Corners was slow. William Wilcox (1781–1820), a tinsmith, had his shop and home at the corner of Washington and Harvard Streets in the early nineteenth century. It was Wilcox who apprenticed Roswell Gleason in this trade. Gleason eventually purchased his former master's business before starting his own business, a Britannia ware factory, at what is now Mother's Rest, just south of Four Corners. He eventually employed upwards of fifty men producing Britannia ware, and later silver-plated teapots, coffeepots, cruets and serving pieces, until the factory was closed in 1871.

With the residential development in the 1890s of the former Tucker estate, Gaylord, Algonquin and Bradley Streets were laid out, and the land was subdivided for building lots. The houses along these streets, all built between

Four Corners is the junction of Washington, Harvard and Bowdoin Streets. The rounded three-story building in the center was built by the Chittenden Brothers as the Mount Bowdoin Market.

1890 and 1920, are substantial examples of Victorian and Colonial Revival architecture. The annexation of Dorchester to Boston in 1870 allowed new residents to live in a planned suburban neighborhood, and the area around Four Corners attracted a diverse group of residents. To serve the needs of this growing neighborhood, Albert and S. Newman Chittenden opened the Mount Bowdoin Market at Four Corners, and Engine 18 built a new firehouse on Harvard Street. Four Corners is a crossroads between Codman Square and Grove Hall, two large shopping districts.

The very name "Four Corners" seems simplistic in regards to an intersection, but I can well remember walking to Four Corners for medicine, to the Chinese laundry with its thick steam rising from the backroom, to visit cousins on Algonquin Street or to borrow books at the Mount Bowdoin Reading Room of the Boston Public Library, just north of the corners.

POPE'S HILL

Pope's Hill was named for William and Frederick Pope, brothers who, in the early nineteenth century, owned a lumberyard at the foot of the hill where the Stop & Shop Supermarket on Morrissey Boulevard is today. William Pope, who lived on the hill and later moved to Commercial (now Freeport) Street, ran the lumberyard in Dorchester. His brother cut, milled and shipped raw timber from Machias, Maine, to Dorchester by barge. The Pope brothers amassed a large fortune, investing heavily in land. By the 1850s, their new lumberyard stretched along the Dorchester waterfront from what is now Victory Road to Freeport Street.

The Neponset area, named after the Massachusetts Indian tribe that once inhabited the region, had only one house prior to 1832, that of the Minot family. The house was at the corner of Neponset Avenue and Chickatawbut Street and was built in the early years of the settlement; it was destroyed by fire in 1872. The Minots were located far from the center of Dorchester. The Indian trail we now know of as Neponset Avenue was the road to the "penny ferry" that crossed to Squantum. The slope of Pope's Hill itself had a somewhat desolate atmosphere until the 1830s, with few houses. In 1833, Josiah Quincy established the Neponset Aqueduct Company to provide fresh water from Pope's Hill to the tollhouse (near Neponset Circle), as the tollhouse was surrounded by salt water. To provide

Pope's Hill, seen in 1880 from Mill Street in Harrison Square, was named for William and Frederick Pope, who owned extensive tracts of land both on the hill and along the Dorchester waterfront. By the mid-nineteenth century, Pope's Hill was developed with magnificent mansions overlooking Dorchester Bay.

this fresh water, Quincy, who was also president of the Neponset Bridge Corporation, which owned the tollhouse and the bridge spanning the Neponset River, constructed a reservoir at the corner of Ashmont and Train Streets. This venture enabled fresh water to be pumped and stored, providing fresh drinking water for the area.

It was an easy commute via the Old Colony Railroad from Pope's Hill to Boston. This ease of transportation triggered the settlement of Pope's Hill, just prior to the Civil War, by affluent families who wished to live in a rural setting but within commuting distance of Boston. The hill was an attractive spot, overlooking Dorchester Bay and the harbor islands, with a panoramic view of the Blue Hills from its summit. In 1858, A.S. Mansfield purchased almost all of the land from Boutwell Street to Claymont Terrace to the summit of the hill. There, Mansfield built an elegant villa overlooking the bay. He also had new streets and house lots laid out and began developing his land. The hill was known at this time as Mansfield Hill in his honor. He later moved to Milton; however, the subdivided estate began to attract new families, among them Lucy Stone and Henry B. Blackwell, who moved

St. Ann's Church was designed by Edward T.P. Graham (1872–1964) and completed in 1920 on the southern slope of Pope's Hill, at the corner of Neponset Avenue and Ashmont Street. By the early twentieth century, Pope's Hill was an attractive neighborhood with a variety of architectural styles.

to Pope's Hill in 1869, just prior to Dorchester's annexation to the city of Boston. Their estate ran the full length of Boutwell Street, on the north side, and faced the large houses of Laban Pratt, the shoe manufacturer; the Frost family, coal suppliers on Commercial Point; and Enoch Train, a wealthy ship owner whose company was known as the Enoch Pratt Line. At the hill's summit was the mansion of Mahlon Spaulding, owner of the Revere Sugar Refinery in Boston. Here, the Spauldings lived in great style in their Italianate mansion, which was later sold to the archdiocese of Boston and converted to the Daly Industrial School for Girls.

The rural aspect of Pope's Hill remained into the early twentieth century, with stately trees shading the streets as mute testimony to the Trains, Pratts, Stone-Blackwells and Spauldings. Today, St. Ann's Roman Catholic Church commands the streetscape at Ashmont Street and Neponset Avenue. Its Italianate bell tower can be seen by passing cars on the Southeast Expressway. Pope's Hill still offers a commanding view of both the harbor and the Blue

Hills, but further development has allowed for more people to enjoy the neighborhood than did a century ago. Pope's Hill has a somewhat newer history than that of other neighborhoods of Dorchester, but the area also has interesting houses of varying architectural styles on streets that echo the past.

CODMAN HILL

Codman Hill in Dorchester was named for the Reverend John Codman, pastor of the Second Church in Dorchester from 1808 to 1847. His home was located on Codman Hill, between Codman Hill and Wilmington Avenues facing Washington Street. Owning over sixty-four acres of land, Codman was one of the few who had houses in this area in the early nineteenth century.

John Codman (1782–1847) was born in Boston and graduated from Harvard College in 1802. Although he studied law after graduation, he was persuaded by his father to become a minister. Leaving for Scotland in 1805, he pursued theological training and became an impressive preacher. When he returned to Boston, he was called to the Second Church in Dorchester to become its new pastor. Codman, though a minister, came from a wealthy family and, after having accepted the position in Dorchester, sought a house. He purchased a large house built by Seth Thayer set high on a terrace above the Upper Road (Washington Street) south of Baker's Corner

Reverend John Codman (1782–1847) was minister of the Second Church in Dorchester, serving from 1808 to 1847. A well-respected man, Codman Square was named in his memory in 1848, and Codman Hill, where his estate was located, also perpetuates his memory.

(now Codman Square). The house was enlarged after Codman's marriage to Mary Wheelwright Codman (1792–1857) and eventually became so large that "ells were succeeded by ells, until, looking at it from the south, it has the unclerical appearance of a rope-walk, or a ten-pin [bowling] alley."

The house, a square Federal mansion with porches on three sides, was set in what formerly had been a silkworm farm. Large numbers of mulberry trees had been imported from Europe and set out to feed the silkworms, which, it was hoped, would produce native silk fibers that would eventually challenge reliance on imported silk. The venture failed; however, many of the mulberry trees survived and surrounded the Codman House. John Codman, who owned roughly the area bounded by Washington, Morton and Torrey Streets and Blue Hill Avenue, had acres of sloping fields, and his house was set high with terraces ascending from the road. The house became a popular stop for visiting ministers who were coming from the countryside to Boston for conventions and were offered hospitality by the Codmans and always made to feel welcome.

Codman experienced great trials when the split between orthodox Congregationalism and Unitarianism occurred. The Second Church opted to remain a Congregational meetinghouse while the First Parish embraced Unitarianism. It was said that "probably in no private dwelling of the land have there been so many doctrinal discussions as in this old mansion house." Codman was beloved not just by his parishioners but also by the entire community. It was said of him that "few men have so rarely erred in judgment and fewer still have found their decisions so justly appreciated while to none has been so freely accorded, at all times, the high praise of just and unprejudiced attention to the business before him." In 1848, the town of Dorchester renamed Baker's Corner, the junction of Washington, Norfolk and Centre Streets and Talbot Avenue, Codman Square in memory of the man who served forty years as pastor of the Second Church. In his will, Codman remembered his former parishioners when he left a tract of land on Norfolk Street to them for use as a parish cemetery.

The Codman House remained the family home until the time of the Civil War, when it was leased to a boarding school for young ladies, first Miss Dodge's School and later Mrs. Cochran's School. The large estate was used as a dairy farm before it was subdivided in the late nineteenth century, and the house remained until it was destroyed by fire in 1928. Today, the relatively new twentieth-century houses on Codman Hill share the same panoramic views of Lower Mills and the Blue Hills that the Codman family once enjoyed.

2

SOCIETIES AND CLUBS

PRINCE HALL LODGE OF MASONS

Prince Hall Grand Lodge is located in Dorchester at 18 Washington Street near Grove Hall. This African American Masonic lodge was founded in 1787 and is the oldest lodge of its kind in this country.

Prince Hall (1735–1807) was born in Barbados, West Indies, to an African American mother and an Englishman. Apprenticed as a young man to learn the trade of the leather worker, he eventually left Barbados and settled in Boston, Massachusetts. Hall was a self-educated man who earned the respect of the African American community in Boston. At the time, African Americans inhabited the western slope of Beacon Hill, and Hall encouraged benevolence and charity toward them. In the years prior to the Revolution, he purchased property, allowing him to vote in all town elections and to voice his opinions at town meetings.

After the Boston Massacre in 1770, Hall and fourteen other "free men of color" were inducted into the Masonic lodge by a group of British soldiers who were quartered at Castle William off the coast of Boston. However, after the Siege of Boston and the evacuation of Loyalists and British soldiers from the city in 1776, Prince Hall organized the first Masonic Lodge for African Americans in this country. Originally, the Masonic order denoted freemasonry, and its members were all skilled masons, but later freemasonry came to be used as a general term meaning that one was a member of a fraternal association for mutual assistance and social enjoyment. In 1784,

Prince Hall (1735–1807) was the founder of the first African American Masonic lodge in America, having been granted a warrant in 1784 by the Grand Lodge of England. A well-respected member of the Boston community, the Prince Hall Grand Lodge of Masons in Grove Hall, Dorchester, perpetuates his memory.

the lodge petitioned the Grand Lodge of England for a warrant, which was granted. The lodge Hall founded for African Americans became quite popular. As first master of this lodge, Hall encouraged other African Americans to join, and he was later successful in organizing African American lodges in Philadelphia and Rhode Island in 1797.

At the time of the Revolution, after the British evacuated Boston, Hall wished to serve his adopted country as a soldier, so he wrote to the committee of safety for the colonies seeking permission to join the Continental army. His petition was approved, and he served under General George Washington. Returning to Boston after the Revolution, Hall became a clergyman and later helped found a school for African American children in Boston. As a respected member of the community, he petitioned the Great and General Court of Massachusetts to support the cause of emancipation and most especially to protect free African Americans in the Boston area from possible kidnapping and eventual sale into slavery in the South.

Prince Hall's life was dedicated to serving his fellow citizens, particularly to championing the rights of African Americans in Boston and offering them a sense of identity and pride. Following his death, the lodge members voted in 1847 to change the name of their lodge to Prince Hall Grand Lodge in memory not only of a loyal master mason but also a respected member of Boston's community.

DORCHESTER WOMAN'S CLUB

After a century of good works and social camaraderie, the Dorchester Woman's Club disbanded in 1995. Though there were few members who supported the club in its final years, it once boasted six hundred members and a magnificent clubhouse and was one of the most active clubs in the State Federation of Women's Clubs.

Founded in 1892 by Clara May Ripley at her home on the corner of Harvard and Bicknell Streets in Dorchester, "three hundred eager women were conferring together, and perfecting an organization which should be broad, simple, and elastic." The club was admitted to the state federation

The Dorchester Woman's Club building was designed by A. Warren Gould and built in 1898 on Centre Street, near Codman Square. With Ripley Hall (on the left) and Whiton Hall, the six-hundred-member club hosted meetings, lectures, dances and musicals. Many Dorchester brides chose to hold their wedding receptions in the elegant clubhouse.

in 1893, and within five years it built its "Air Castle," a high-style Georgian Revival clubhouse designed by local architect A. Warren Gould, who also happened to be the husband of member Susie Gould. The clubhouse was composed of Whiton Hall, named for club president Ella Whiton, and Ripley Hall, named for founder Clara Ripley. The first meeting in the new clubhouse was held in November 1898, and each member paid sixty-nine cents for her chair.

Because the situation of women a century ago was marked by much greater inequality than it is today, the Dorchester Woman's Club was much less involved in town affairs and far from financially self-sufficient. However, the club was composed of energetic, educated and concerned women of Dorchester using the seal of the town of Dorchester and the motto signifying piety, learning and industry (the three virtues of the Puritans who settled Dorchester in 1630). The members of the club "maintained the custom first established, and presented annually sixteen programs. Stimulating to the thought, the sympathies, or the artistic sense of the attending members, and catering at times to their palates as well, since even women grow wondrous open-hearted over their teacups." With lectures, art shows, musicals and evening dances, the Dorchester Woman's Club became one of the most successful clubs of its kind in the Greater Boston area.

In the early twentieth century, the club also sponsored community development, social services and visits to hospitals. In 1913, musical instruments were donated to the Dorchester High School Regiment, with ten bugles and fourteen snare drums emblazoned with the name and seal of the club. To further young adults, the merit scholarship was established in 1915 for college-bound Dorchesterites and is still awarded by the state federation. Throughout the twentieth century, though a social club in nature, the Dorchester Woman's Club sponsored good will and service to the community. Hand-knitted afghans were donated to the Carney Hospital for children during the holiday season. With bazaars and open houses in the 1940 to 1960 period, the club maintained full membership, but as more women sought employment, membership began to dwindle after 1960. Many women were unable to give the time to an organization that met during the day or to assist in the sundry duties of maintaining a large clubhouse where many weddings and shower receptions were held for decades.

The last decade of the club's existence saw the membership drop to fewer than thirty members, most of whom were either past presidents or longtime members who loyally supported the club, often from far-flung towns. The days of dances and musical afternoons had passed, as had the need for Whiton and Ripley Halls, and the clubhouse was sold to Doyle's Catering Company. A short return to the elegance of 1898 was witnessed when Whiton Hall opened for Sunday brunch in the early 1980s. The remaining club members, who were heard to remark how good the clubhouse still looked, attended a reception for the 100th anniversary of the Dorchester Woman's Club but were unable to continue the club. The former clubhouse is now the New Life Restoration Temple.

Today, we remember the Dorchester Woman's Club as an important social institution in Dorchester with dance classes for children, a local history class for club members, wedding receptions and myriad activities that made the clubhouse come to life.

Dorchester Gentlemen's Driving Club

Franklin Field, located at the corner of Blue Hill and Talbot Avenues, is not as vast an open area as it was in the late nineteenth century. Still, it creates a dramatic vista in the densely settled area just west of Codman Square. In the 1930s, the area was a favorite promenade on Sunday afternoons when families walked to Franklin Field for socials and children frolicked in the field. When I was a child, fireworks were set off at Franklin Field during Dorchester Day, and we ogled at their brilliance as we watched from our family's third-floor observatory. However, at the turn of the twentieth century, Franklin Field was the site of the driving course of the Dorchester Gentlemen's Driving Club.

The Dorchester Gentlemen's Driving Club was chartered in 1890 but was not organized until 1899 at a meeting held in the stable of Hollis Gallup on Barnes Street in Dorchester. The club was composed of men who enjoyed racing their horses in a competitive manner for awards and recognition. The first president was Charles L. Young, and the club was "the first driving club in this country whose by-laws and constitution called for weekly meeting of its members and weekly racing of horses for ribbons." The club membership was largely composed of Dorchesterites and proved an immediate success. Originally, the weekly races were held on Blue Hill Avenue, between Talbot Avenue and Callender Street, on a "quarter-mile speedway that had been

The racecourse and the wood-framed starter's tower of the Dorchester Gentlemen's Driving Club were at Franklin Field, at the corner of Talbot and Blue Hill Avenues. The club was composed of men who enjoyed racing their horses in a competitive manner for awards and recognition.

granted the club by the city and which was kept in fine condition for racing by money secured from among the members, many of whom went down into their pockets for as high as $25 each."

Slowly, the land around Franklin Field was developed for residential use. As Blue Hill Avenue became more active with traffic, the members of the club petitioned the City of Boston to allow them to grade a portion of Franklin Field for a speedway and grandstand. By 1911, the new speedway was completed, and a large celebration was planned, with Mayor John "Honey Fitz" Fitzgerald leading a parade of sulkies down Talbot Avenue from Codman Square to the new half-mile speedway. A popular club, "the Dorchester Gentlemen's Driving Club was the leading social club in the Dorchester district, and if 'by the works thou shalt be known,' the speedway of Franklin Field stands as a monument to the power of these members as a political organization."

The weekly races, in which members raced horses attached to one-seated sulkies, were never more popular than during the festivities of Dorchester Day. In 1912, Mayor Fitzgerald, the father of Rose Fitzgerald Kennedy (and thus the maternal grandfather of future United States president John F. Kennedy), who lived on Welles Avenue near Codman Square, participated in the races and won. He was presented with a large silver cup by Councilor Collins for his win, and after receiving his cup, he entertained those in attendance with his trademark song, "Sweet Adeline." It is said in the club's records that on this day, over fifteen thousand people attended the races and participated in the activities of Dorchester Day.

The club competed with other driving clubs around Boston, among them the Lynn Driving Club, the Old Colony Driving Club in South Weymouth, the Metropolitan Driving Club in Boston and the Quannapowitt Driving Club in Reading. Competition was always conducted in the best of spirits. At a race in Readville, a part of the town of Hyde Park that was later annexed to Boston in 1912, in 1901, the Dorchester Gentlemen's Driving Club "staged the first handicap race for harness horses ever given in this country." As the need for horses began to wane in the first decade of the twentieth century with the ascendancy of the automobile, the driving club's membership began to decrease. Still, for nearly two decades Dorchesterites created good-hearted fun and excitement at the Franklin Field Speedway.

FRANKLIN PARK GOLF COURSE

Webster's Dictionary describes golf as "an outdoor game played with a set of clubs and a ball, in which the ball is driven with the fewest strokes into a succession of holes." Simple enough; however, when the first game of golf was played in Dorchester in 1890, few rules, let alone residents, existed to explain the new outdoor phenomenon.

Golf was invented in Scotland, and the mecca of golf is considered to be St. Andrews, where the Royal and Ancient Golf Club of Saint Andrews was founded in the seventeenth century. For a long time, it seemed to be a wholly British sport. Even in the last decade of the nineteenth century, few Americans had heard of or participated in the sport. In Boston at that time, the firm of Wright & Ditson supplied much of the sporting equipment used by local athletes. The firm imported cricket bats and balls, which sold well, but a principal in the British export firm decided to include golf clubs and a dozen golf balls with an order sent from England. When the golf clubs arrived, they came without instructions, and neither George Wright, nor anyone he knew, understood the game. As a result, the golf clubs were put on a shelf, where they sat until the fall of 1890.

The Golf House at Franklin Park was a stone pavilion with a red-tiled roof designed by Edmund March Wheelwright (1854–1912), city of Boston architect.

George Wright (1847–1937), for whom a golf course was later named in Hyde Park, was a pioneer in the sport of baseball. He played shortstop for the original Cincinnati Red Stockings, the first fully professional team, when he was perhaps the game's best player. In 1868, Wright won the Clipper Medal for being the best shortstop in baseball. He was inducted into the Baseball Hall of Fame in 1937. He was a partner at Wright & Ditson Sporting Goods in Boston and decided to exhibit a few golf clubs and balls in a window display. Though he didn't know how to play the game, it obviously made for an eye-catching window display. He is quoted in *Fifty Years of American Golf*, by Harry Brownlow Martin, as saying:

> *One day a Scotchman passed the store and noticing the clubs came in and asked where he could find a golf course. I told him that we had no course, but explained how we happened to have the clubs. The Scotchman became interested and sketched on a piece of paper how a course should be laid out and gave a description of the game. About a week later I received from him a book of rules with pictures of a full set of clubs and their names underneath.*

Excited, George Wright looked for an open space to play golf, and he seized on the open rolling land at Franklin Park, recently laid out by Frederick Law Olmsted. When he started to dig holes, a policeman informed Wright that he required a permit from the Boston Park Commissioners to play golf at Franklin Park. After applying for the permit in writing, the commissioners denied permission due to the danger of people being hurt by flying balls.

An early twentieth-century golfer is seen after hitting his golf ball on the fairway. What was a fairly unknown game in 1890 was to become one enjoyed by golfers of every level, all thanks to sportsman George Wright (1847–1937).

Undaunted, Wright petitioned the commissioners in person and succeeded in securing the required permit. Consequently, in the fall of 1890, George Wright and his friend John Smith went to the southern slope of Franklin Park and laid out holes with a yardstick fashioned with a red flannel pennant for flags. With this crude, makeshift course, Wright and a group of his friends enjoyed the first game of golf in Boston. Not only were these first golf players in Boston destined to create a trend, but it was also, according to *Fifty Years of American Golf*, "undoubtedly…the first golf ever played in a public park in this country."

The William J. Devine Golf Course at Franklin Park was officially established in 1896 and is considered the second-oldest public golf course in the nation, the first being behind Van Cortlandt Park in the Bronx of New York City. An eighteen-hole golf course, it was designed by Donald J. Ross, ASGCA, one of the foremost designers of golf courses in the twentieth century.

Today, over a century later, the Franklin Park golf course, so crudely laid out by George Wright, can once again be enjoyed by golfers. Drive through the park any weekend morning and you will see dozens of golfers enjoying the clean air and impressive open vistas available in the heart of the city. The course is under the direction of the city of Boston's Parks and Recreation Department and has a rich legacy that will ensure its place in the history of golf.

3

ARTISTS, AUTHORS AND ACTIVISTS

CHILDE HASSAM

Childe Hassam is considered to be among the finest of the American Impressionist painters, and his oils and watercolors bring six-digit figures in the leading auction houses of this country. However, few realize that he was born and raised in Dorchester.

Frederick Childe Hassam (1859–1935) was born on Olney Street on Meeting House Hill, the son of Frederick Fitch and Rosa Hawthorne Hassam. The house was a small cottage with a stable in the rear and still stands amidst modern structures. His mother was related to Nathaniel Hawthorne, the noted nineteenth-century writer, and his father was descended from the Horsham family, as the name was originally spelled. Hassam attended the Mather School on Meeting House Hill and later Dorchester High School, when it was located at the corner of Dorchester Avenue and Gibson Street. He left school in 1876 to apprentice in the shop of George E. Johnson, a wood engraver at 9 Milk Street in Boston.

As a child, Hassam had shown keen ability in the art of watercolor, and according to Donelson Hoopes, one of his many biographers, Hassam

> *remembered copying the sporting prints in the billiard room of the family house on Olney Street, and using an old coach parked in the backyard for a studio. His first recollection of an original work of art, other than his own, was that of Thomas Hewes Hinckley, a painter of sentimental animal subjects who lived in the nearby town of Milton.*

Childe Hassam (1859–1935) seems deep in thought in this photograph from the 1890s. Well dressed in a wool suit and beret, he holds a brush in one hand, and an unfinished watercolor rests on the chair in front of him. Hassam was a founder of the Ten American Painters, a group of artists who personified the Impressionist movement in America.

As a result, Hassam was largely self-taught prior to joining Johnson's studio, and he had a sharp eye for engravings and graphic media. He freelanced as an illustrator during the 1875 to 1885 period and designed covers for *Harper's Weekly*, the *Marblehead Messenger*, the *Century* and *Scribner's*. Not only was Hassam sought as an engraver, but also his watercolors were commissioned for William Dean Howell's *Venetian Life* and Celia Thaxter's *An Island Garden*, two immensely popular books that are still appreciated and are included in my own library.

In the late 1870s, Hassam began formalized art lessons in Boston, joining the Boston Art Club's evening art classes while working days as an illustrator. His painting style began to develop as impressionistic, especially under the

The Charles River and Beacon Hill was painted by Childe Hassam in 1892 and depicts the embankment (later to become Storrow Drive) that paralleled the Charles River. The gilded dome of the Massachusetts State House can be seen in the distance with the unfinished riverfront of the Back Bay. *Collection of the Museum of Fine Arts, Boston.*

tutoring of Ignaz Marcel Gaugengigl (1855–1932), who arrived in Boston from Bavaria in the 1880s. This master of the realist movement imparted to Childe Hassam, as he was now known at the suggestion of Celia Thaxter, the respect for form while veiling the subject with paint strokes. Through both Gaugengigl and William Rimmer, a medical doctor, painter, sculptor and anatomical illustrator from Milton, Hassam was developing a style of painting that came to be classified as the Boston School. His painting style continued to develop, but it was his first trip to Europe in 1883 that allowed his creativity to absorb the old masters. After a yearlong trip through Britain, the Netherlands, Brittany, Italy and Spain, he returned to Boston to show sixty-seven of his European watercolors at the gallery of Williams and Everett on Park Street in Boston.

As his artistic career began to take on importance, in 1884 he proposed to and married Kathleen Maude Doan of Dorchester. They moved to New York City, where Hassam set up a studio on the West Side. He continued to pursue his study of art and was accepted to display his art at the Paris Salon in both 1887 and 1888, showing the first signs of his impressionistic sense of art. Impressionism had developed in France with the attempt at an impression that the eye and mind gather rather than representing the actual fact. Hassam became a master of this revolutionary art form and was awarded medals from the Boston Art Club, the National Academy of Design, the Columbian Exposition, the Pan-American Exposition, the Universal Exposition in St. Louis and the Exposition Universelle, Paris.

His art was lauded, and actively collected, throughout the world, and he continued to serve the art world through the founding, in 1889, of the

A detail of *Boston Common at Twilight* by Childe Hassam shows a mother and her daughters feeding birds on the Tremont Street side of the Boston Common, with a busy streetscape of pedestrians and streetcars and a buttery sunset mottling a snow-covered park at twilight. *Collection of the Museum of Fine Arts, Boston.*

New York Watercolor Society, of which he was the first president. He later joined the Pastel Society. He also formed the Ten American Painters, an exclusive club of friends and fellow artists who personified the Impressionist movement in America. His fellow members were Frank Benson, Joseph R. De Camp, T.W. Dewing, W.L. Metcalf, R. Reid, E.E. Simmons, Edmund Tarbell, A.A. Weir and Joseph H. Twachtman. These were the "movers and shakers" of American art in the late nineteenth century, and they drew inspiration from one another in addition to changing the attitudes toward art for the Victorian era.

In 1926, Hassam was asked to display his art at a retrospective exhibit at the Durand-Ruel Gallery in New York. Not only was this fifty-year retrospective well attended, but it also served to reinforce Hassam's vast contributions to the art world. His creativity was recognized in the presentation of the Gold Medal for Distinguished Services to the Fine Arts by the Association of American Art Dealers. Hassam was well respected but could well remember his youth in Dorchester when he was a struggling art student. Knowing that there would always be aspiring art students in need of financial assistance, he established a fund to aid them and called it the Hassam Fund, naming it in honor of his wife, Maude Doan Hassam. His death in 1935 in East Hampton, Long Island, New York, was not unexpected, but with him went a talent that few could emulate let alone match. That year, he was awarded the Saltus Medal for Merit by the National Academy in recognition for his achievements. In 1936, Childe Hassam was inducted posthumously into the American Academy of Arts and Letters.

The entire town of Dorchester can share in the pride and achievement of a native son. His art will endure as that of a genius—a Dorchester genius.

Elisha Brown Bird

Bookplates might be thought of as a luxury few of us can afford, but a century ago, a book without the owner's name and plate might never be returned. Though most bookplates would simply state that it was *Ex Libris*, from someone's library, one Dorchester resident took them to new heights.

Elisha Brown Bird (1868–1943) was the son of John and Rebecca Richardson Bird, whose house was on West Cottage Street, the present site of NSTAR Electric. Educated at the Massachusetts Institute of Technology,

Elisha Brown Bird (1868–1943) was a noted "Book Plate Designer," as he called himself, who was said by the American Antiquarian Society to be among the four most important bookplate designers living in the 1920s.

Bird was later employed at the *Boston Herald* as a cartoonist to sketch baseball games while in progress. This new form of "reporting" allowed him to perfect his quick sketches, but his artistic skills were not being challenged. He was later to establish an office where he created bookplates for noted collectors. Within a few years, Elisha Brown Bird, "Book Plate Designer," as he called himself, published a collection of bookplates in "photogravure" for prospective clients. Printed in 1916, this collection included the bookplates of the Bostonian Society, Wellesley College, the New Bedford Public Library and numerous private collections. So artistic and unique had his bookplates become that "when the American Antiquarian Society decided to make a collection of the best American bookplates in the 20s, they chose works from only four of the then living bookplate men: Messrs. Hofsen, Mac Donald, Smith and artist Elisha B. Bird from Dorchester, Massachusetts," according to an article by Curtis Norris in the October 1972 edition of *Yankee* magazine.

By the 1930s, bookplates, which "are not a luxury but a necessity for the man who desires to beautify his library," had become Bird's mission in life. According to an article in 1934, "It takes Mr. Bird about a week to turn out a bookplate design. He does most of the work with pen and pencil. The

Elisha Brown Bird designed his own bookplate, using a cavalier, replete with a lace collar and high leather boots, lounging in a great chair, engrossed in reading a book. Bird said that bookplates "are not a luxury but a necessity for a man who desires to beautify his library."

original is about eight by twelve inches, but this is reduced to four by two and three-eighths on the plate." It has been said that his entire life was dedicated to creative art and that his experience in the newspaper field included such well-known newspapers as the *Boston Globe*, the *Boston Herald*, the *Boston Transcript* and the *New York World*, *Times* and *Evening Post*.

Later in life, Bird designed bookplates for the Massachusetts Institute of Technology, Knox College, Princeton University, Yale University and the College of William and Mary. His bookplates for personal libraries included those of Jessica Dragonette, "the Muse of Song"; Charles H. Taylor, founder of the *Boston Globe*; Frank Wood, for whom the Wood Nursing Home on Morton Street was named; and my own grandfather. In a press release, the *Ex-Libris Journal* in London said:

> Mr. Bird's drawings are unusually strong black and white...and always show careful thought in their...execution. They show the hand of a master artist in the excellence of drawing and figure work, and in the conception of color and tone.

Upon his death in 1943, his obituary read, "Elisha Brown Bird, internationally known illustrator and many years president of the American Society of Bookplate Designers and Collectors died this morning." His bookplates continue to identify not just the owners of the books they are pasted into but also a Dorchester artist who was considered to be among the finest in his field.

LUCY STONE

Lucy Stone (1818–1893), well known for her writings and activism in women's rights and the abolition of slavery, was a longtime resident of Pope's Hill in Dorchester. Stone was born in North Brookfield, Massachusetts, the daughter of farmers who traced their descent from early English settlers. Her early youth was somewhat uneventful, but after entering Oberlin College in Oberlin, Ohio, her life became one of

Lucy Stone (1818–1893) was the first Massachusetts woman to be awarded a college degree, the first woman to retain her maiden name after marriage, the first female editor (the *Woman's Journal*) and, following her death, the first person to be cremated in New England. A role model for women in the United States, the city of Boston built a school designed by Frank I. Cooper near Codman Square in 1937 and named it in her memory.

dedication and service to the causes of abolition and women's rights and to becoming a consummate political organizer.

Lucy Stone worked her way through Oberlin College by doing odd jobs and, upon graduation in 1847, was the first Massachusetts woman to have been awarded a college degree. As Oberlin was on the Underground Railroad, which took slaves north to freedom, she learned about the horrors of slavery. Her involvement with the antislavery movement led to her marriage to Henry Brown Blackwell, an ardent abolitionist from Cincinnati, Ohio. After their marriage in 1855, Stone maintained her maiden name, the first time in recorded history of such an act.

Blackwell was from a prominent family with its own firsts. His sisters were Dr. Elizabeth Blackwell, the first woman to graduate from medical school, and Dr. Emily Blackwell, the third woman in this country to receive a medical degree; his sister-in-law was Reverend Antoinette Brown Blackwell, the first woman ordained as a minister in this country. With such illustrious company, Stone thrived. In 1867, accompanied by her husband, Stone attended the Kansas Impartial Suffrage Association, which led to the formation of the

The Stone-Blackwell House was an impressive Italianate house on Boutwell Street on Pope's Hill. Lucy Stone and Henry Brown Blackwell purchased it in 1869, the year Dorchester voted to annex itself to Boston.

Woman's Journal, a weekly newspaper she was to edit until her death. In 1869, she assisted in the founding of the Woman's Suffrage Association of America, where she served as president until 1872. Her husband and daughter, Alice Stone Blackwell, continued the publication until 1930, without missing a single week. With her career as solid as one could hope for, the family moved to Pope's Hill in Dorchester in 1869, the year the town residents voted in favor of annexation to the city of Boston. The sharply rising hill was a rural area that was accessible to the city. The house they purchased was built in the Italianate style about 1860 and overlooked Dorchester Bay.

Stone died in 1893; in attendance was Dr. William Cranch Bond Fifield, husband of Emily Fifield, the second female member of the Boston School Committee. Stone was cremated at the New England Cremation Society (now the Forest Hills Cemetery). Her family lived on at the house on Pope's Hill until Henry Blackwell died in 1909. After her father's death, Alice Stone Blackwell moved to an apartment building, the Monadnock, on Dudley Street in Upham's Corner. She then arranged for the Pope's Hill house to be deeded to the Lucy Stone Home, a benevolent corporation that was to allow underprivileged inner-city residents to partake of the country estate, which still had a rural flavor in 1919. Later, the Boutwell Street house was deeded to the Morgan Memorial, which used it for similar purposes until it was destroyed by fire in 1971.

The City of Boston built the Lucy Stone School in 1937 at 22 Regina Road in Dorchester, which was designed by the Frank I. Cooper Corporation. Lucy Stone was fittingly inducted into the National Women's Hall of Fame, located in Seneca Falls, New York, on International Women's Day, March 8, 1986.

MARIA CUMMINS

The concept of social reform and responsibility was a great factor in the behavior of many nineteenth-century Dorchesterites, and no person was more aware of this than Miss Cummins.

Maria Susanna Cummins (1827–1866) was born in Salem, Massachusetts, the daughter of the Honorable David and Maria Franklin Kittredge Cummins; her father was the judge of common pleas in Norfolk County. She was educated at the exclusive Mrs. Sedgwick's School in Lenox, returning to

Maria Susanna Cummins (1827–1866) was the noted authoress of *The Lamplighter*, one of the most popular books in the 1850s, having sold an astonishing sixty-five thousand copies in five months. She was said to have been highly religious, "endowed with… refined and gentle qualities," and was beloved by all who knew her.

her father's home in Dorchester after her "finishing." The Cumminses were a well-to-do family of education and wealth who had moved to Dorchester's Meeting House Hill in the 1840s. The Cummins family had purchased the former Turks Head Tavern on Bowdoin Street, an eighteenth-century tavern that was built by Reverend John Danforth, minister of the Dorchester Meeting House, in 1712. Once the family had settled, they began to attend the First Parish Church on Meeting House Hill, and Maria Cummins began to teach Sunday school at the church, where interestingly the first Sunday school class had been formed in 1822, one of the first Unitarian classes in the area. Under the direction of William Taylor Adams (known by his nom de plume, Oliver Optic), Miss Cummins led a defined and religious life, devoting herself to her students.

The Cummins House was built in 1712 by Reverend John Danforth (1660–1730) and in 1732 became the popular Turks Head Tavern. The house was sketched in 1868 by Dorchester resident Paul S. Yendell, an artist, "an independent amateur variable star astronomer" and author of *Observation of Variable Stars*.

Reverend Theodore Clapp said of her in 1854:

> *No lady of my acquaintance is more richly endowed with those mild, social, refined and gentle qualities which, in view of our sex, generally, constitute the principal beauty of the female character…* [and that] *simplicity is the crowning ornament to her manners, as well as her writings.*

In 1850, she undertook the writing of a novel to please her nieces, the daughters of her sister Helen and Edmund Pitt Tileston. Helen Cummins had married Edmund Pitt Tileston, co-owner of the Tileston & Hollingsworth Paper Mill on the Neponset River. He was a founder, in 1843, the year of his marriage, of the Dorchester Historical and Antiquarian Society and was active in numerous charities. Their daughters, Florence, Grace and Katherine Tileston, were doted upon by their aunt, and with the publication in 1853 of her book, *The Lamplighter*, they were flattered by the attention.

Published anonymously, the book sold over sixty-five thousand copies within five months. The novel went through numerous editions and was used in many Unitarian Sunday school classes throughout New England.

In the period between 1850 and her death in 1866, Miss Cummins wrote *Mabel Vaughan*, *El Fureidis*, *Little Gerty* and *Haunted Hearts*. She also contributed numerous articles for the prestigious *Atlantic Monthly*. The books were all of a semireligious type and were well received by her readers. Of a deeply religious nature herself, Maria Cummins joined the First Parish Church in 1864. She died after a lengthy illness and was to be buried from the church on Meeting House Hill on October 1, 1866, and interred in her family's lot at Forest Hills Cemetery.

ROBERT BALL HUGHES

Robert Ball Hughes (1806–1868) was an eminent nineteenth-century sculptor who once lived on School Street opposite Mother's Rest in Dorchester. Known for his skill as a sculptor, he was also remarkably adept at painting, wax portraiture and etching. Robert Ball Hughes was born in London,

Robert Ball Hughes (1806–1868) was an eminently gifted sculptor and artist who lived on School Street near Four Corners.
A fine artist, he was equally temperamental and displayed his obvious talent better while "under the influence."

England, and as a young child showed marked aptitude in modeling figures from the family's supply of wax candles. His figures were thought to be so well formed that he was enrolled in the Royal Academy. He later entered the studio of Edward Hodges Bailey, a noted sculptor in London, and exhibited his works at the Royal Academy.

Ball Hughes married in London and in 1829 set sail for New York with his new wife, Georgianna Ball Hughes. Once in New York City, he opened his own studio and began to receive the attention of the city. His first major commission was a statue of the late governor De Witt Clinton. He was later given the commission to sculpt a statue of Alexander Hamilton for the Rotunda of the Merchants Exchange in New York. The statue, thought to be the first marble portrait sculpture in America, was destroyed in 1835 by fire eight months after it was completed. His grief must have been great, and he and his family removed to Philadelphia.

In Philadelphia, Ball Hughes competed for the commission of an equestrian statue of President George Washington. His model was thought to be the finest submitted for consideration, and it was said that "in Mr. Hughes' design we see everything to admire, and nothing to condemn." The model showed the president astride a noble horse, bowing with his hat to his assembled constituents. The design was selected by the committee above all other entries; however, the failure of the Bank of the United States in 1841 ended the project's funding and thus the commission. Dejected, Ball Hughes left with his family for Boston, and he settled in the town of Dorchester on Adams Street in Cedar Grove, opposite what is now the Cedar Grove Cemetery. Known as Gin Plain in the early nineteenth century, this area was a large, flat plain that overlooked the Neponset River. The area was a favorite spot for walking, and the Ball Hugheses must have enjoyed the rural setting after such bad luck in New York and Philadelphia. Robert Ball Hughes continued his sculpting, producing busts of Washington Irving in 1836 and Edward Livingston in 1838 and a large seated portrait of Nathaniel Bowditch, the noted navigator. This model was later to become the bronze memorial of Bowditch at Mount Auburn Cemetery. His work continued to be sought out, but his career, initially so successful, began to slowly dwindle.

The family moved about 1851 to School Street between Codman Square and Four Corners. The house was originally built by Captain Jeremiah Spaulding, a well-known shipmaster in the East India trade. His wife and their daughters, Augusta and Georgianna, lived in simple comfort while Ball

Hughes began to teach art, lecture locally and develop a new form of art, that of "poker sketches," whereby a hot poker is drawn along a piece of wood to create a design by the singeing of the wood. These peculiar forms of art were so popular that the artist created a series, including *The Trumpeter, The Monk, Falstaff Examining His Recruits, Rembrandt, Shakespeare, Rubens* and *Don Quixote*. These pieces, though not as time-consuming as sculpting, continued to provide an income for the family.

Robert Ball Hughes was undoubtedly a fine artist but a highly temperamental one. It is recorded that he displayed his talent better while "under the influence." His ability to create a likeness, be it in clay, marble or even a subject to be painted (he painted portraits to augment his income), made Ball Hughes an exceptional artist. His death in 1868 left a void in the world of art. Through disappointments, destruction of his art and misfortune, he never attained the success or recognition that an artist of his ability should have enjoyed. The home of the Ball Hughes family, known as Sunnyside, still stands on School Street and was the home of his widow for many years. Their daughter Georgianna never married; she inherited a large measure of her father's artistic ability, continuing the artistic environment that her father created and nurtured.

Robert Ball Hughes was buried in the newly laid-out Cedar Grove Cemetery a year after it was established. His grave overlooks the Neponset River and has a panoramic view from its knoll. His artistic genius, though never fully utilized, flourished in his Dorchester studio.

JOHN LOTHROP MOTLEY

John Lothrop Motley (1814–1877) was a noted historian of the nineteenth century. He was born in Dorchester, Massachusetts, and died in Dorchester, Dorset, England. The son of Thomas Motley, he was born at the corner of Adams and Centre Streets. The Motleys lived in a Federal house and propagated numerous fruit trees in the garden. John's brother, Thomas Motley, was later elected president of the Massachusetts Society for the Promotion of Agriculture.

Motley was educated at the school on Meeting House Hill (now the Mather School) and graduated from Harvard College in 1831. He then studied in Germany, gaining fluency in the language, and furthered his education at

John Lothrop Motley (1814–1877) was a noted historian whose work was so highly regarded that he was posthumously elected to the Hall of Fame for Great Americans in 1910. The City of Boston, in 1911, dedicated a public school to his memory on Savin Hill Avenue in Dorchester.

the Universities of Gottingen and Berlin, studying law. Motley returned to Dorchester in 1833 and studied law, but he never practiced in the profession. In 1841, he was sent to St. Petersburg in Russia as secretary to the delegation for the United States Embassy. Staying there only a few years, he returned to Boston in 1845 to pursue a writing career. His first published work was a long article on the life of Peter the Great, which must have been the result of his sojourn in Russia. In 1856, at his own expense, he published a three-volume history of the Netherlands, *The Rise of the Dutch Republic*. It was hailed as an important work pertaining to the Dutch rebellion against Spain during the sixteenth century. It proved so popular that it was translated into Dutch, German, French and Russian. Between 1860 and 1867, Motley published a four-volume edition of *The History of the United Netherlands*. He also to published *Merry Mount, A Romance of the Massachusetts Colony*, proving that he was a historian not solely immersed in the lore and attraction of Europe.

After publishing a series of articles in the *London Times* explaining the situation of the Civil War in this country and outlining how the problem of slavery compounded the situation, he was appointed ambassador to the court of Saint James, the highest honor a diplomat from this country could receive. President Abraham Lincoln's appointment of Motley ensured that our representation in Great Britain would be professional, but it was volatile in regards to the political ramifications of the war. Motley was recalled in 1867 by President Ulysses Grant, whose political alignments sharply differed from those of Motley. He returned to Boston, settling on Beacon Hill, and contented himself with the publication of *The Life and Death of John of Barneveld*, which dealt with the hero of the Thirty Years' War.

After his death, Motley was thought sufficiently important to be elected to the Hall of Fame for Great Americans in 1910. The City of Boston, through the Boston School Committee, designed and built, in 1911, the John Lothrop Motley School on Savin Hill Avenue in Dorchester to commemorate him as an eminent historian and one of the most important Dorchesterites of his generation. The school, which served the education needs of four generations of children from Savin Hill, was closed in the late 1970s and subsequently converted into condominiums.

John Lothrop Motley's research and writing endures to this day; a set of handsomely bound volumes graces my own library. Dorchester history, and those of us involved in preserving it, never ceases to reward the inquisitive of mind with the discoveries of Dorchester people and events that have influenced the world.

THEODORE WHITE

In the first chapter of Theodore White's book *In Search of History*, he describes in vivid detail his youth in Dorchester in the early twentieth century. The chapter "Exercise in Recollection" creates a vivid impression of an immigrant's viewpoint of a town settled by Puritans escaping the Old World and creating a new society based on the Augustinian view of a "City Upon a Hill." White, however, gives us a childhood in Dorchester from the viewpoint of an American citizen born to Russian Jews. Theodore White (1915–1986) was born on Erie Street, a nondescript street adjacent to the Midlands Branch of the New York, New Haven & Hartford Railroad. Near his home was Grove Hall, a bustling shopping district that once boasted a magnificent estate, Grove Hall, for which the intersection of Blue Hill Avenue and Warren and Washington Streets was named.

Dorchester changed dramatically after it was annexed to the city of Boston in 1870, and White recounted that Erie Street was then a bustling market street ancillary to the main shopping artery of Blue Hill Avenue: "Storekeepers had transformed Erie Street from the quiet residential neighborhood my grandparents had sought as Jewish pioneers in the district to a supermarket bazaar." The presence of immigrants in Dorchester was an important factor in the development of the town, for Dorchester's proximity to Boston allowed for both the affluent and those less fortunate to enjoy the same amenities. Both the descendants of the Puritans and the newer arrivals from Eastern Europe experienced the same cool breezes from Dorchester Bay during the summer,

Theodore White (1915–1986) was a noted historian and successful author who was born on Erie Street in Dorchester. A noted journalist and Pulitzer Prize–winning author, White wrote lovingly of his childhood in Dorchester in his book *In Search of History*.

the same panoramic views of the harbor and the Blue Hills and the same enjoyment of the exotic animals at Franklin Park Zoo. The streets radiating from the Upper Road (now Washington Street) attracted ethnic enclaves that had distinct connotations from Irish, Jewish or German settlements. White spoke of inner-city neighborhoods as being part of a ballet that is different in each city. He said that "in the larger cosmopolitan cities of the Eastern Seaboard, old stock Protestants gave way to the Irish, who gave way in turn to Italians or Jews, who gave way in turn to blacks."

However, being the grandchild of Eastern European Jews separated White from his contemporaries. He lived with his family in a two-family house that had been purchased for $2,000 in 1912, in a neighborhood that had once attracted more affluent residents. The house, unprepossessing by today's standards, was an important feature in his youth, as

> *the house on Erie Street connected me, unknowingly, directly to the New England past. It might have been gardened by John Greenleaf Whittier, and its garden was the most beautiful on the block. All the New England flowers about which I read in school, in the poems of Longfellow, and Whittier, and Emerson, and in the stories of Thornton Burgess, grew in my own backyard. Under the lilac bushes grew lilies of the valley; we continued to replant the tiger lilies and tulips until we became too poor to buy tulip bulbs. To the original fruit trees, a pear and a cherry, my grandmother added a peach tree and a grapevine.*

Erie Street, carved out of the lands surrounding the former Atherton estate, was an attractive neighborhood. Tree-lined streets and a pleasant walk to Franklin Park must have sparked White's imagination, but it was Miss Fuller, his sixth-grade teacher at the Gibson School on Mount Bowdoin, who "set fire to the imagination of the ordinary children who sat in lumps before her, and to do so was probably the chief reward she sought." However, the public school education received by the children of immigrants could prove confusing, for the poems and stories read in school could be in marked contrast to the sounds of street merchants leading their

> *horse-and-wagons through Erie Street; they would yodel and chant their wares. For each peddler another chant: the fish man would sing in a special voice "Lebediker fisch, weiber, Lebediker fisch"; the secondhand-clothes*

merchant would chant otherwise; the Italian banana man would chorus only "Bananas, bananas, bananas," hawking a fruit previously unknown to Eastern Europeans.

Though a noted journalist and Pulitzer Prize–winning author, Theodore White once curiously said that Jews have no place at all in the grand history of Western thought, but the courage his own family showed in their immigration from Russia to Dorchester proved so interesting that his book remains a familiar and deeply personal adventure of an immigrant group in Dorchester in the early twentieth century.

4
FELLOW TOWNSWOMEN
OF DORCHESTER

ELIDA RUMSEY FOWLE

Elida Rumsey Fowle (1843–1919) was known during the Civil War as the "Songbird of the North," as she entertained Union soldiers with rousing patriotic songs and is reputed to have been the first to sing in public Julia Ward Howe's anthem "The Battle Hymn of the Republic."

The Rumseys moved to Washington, D.C., from Tarrytown, New York, in 1861, and Miss Rumsey gave informal concerts at her family's home on Judiciary Square. Popular, she was one of a quartet asked to sing for Sunday services at the House of Representatives. It was here that she met her future husband, John Allan Fowle of Boston. After services, the two began to visit hospitals in the vicinity, giving religious tracts from the American Tract Society and homemade jellies and cakes to recuperating Union soldiers. Many times, Elida was induced to sing such songs as "The Rebel Flags" and "The Dying Soldier Boy," songs written by Fowle expressly for Elida Rumsey.

After a short courtship, the two were married in the House of Representatives by Chaplain Alonzo Quint, the minister who held services there on Sunday mornings. They were married in 1863 with almost four thousand people attending their wedding. With members of Congress, the Senate and numerous Union soldiers who were recipients of their largess, it is still the only wedding to have taken place in the congressional chambers. With a request from the gallery, Elida Rumsey Fowle stood on the desk of the Speaker of the House and sang "The Battle Hymn of the Republic."

Elida Rumsey Fowle (1843–1919) was known as the "Songbird of the North" for her sweet singing during the Civil War. She was the first to sing in public Julia Ward Howe's anthem "The Battle Hymn of the Republic" and was married to John Allan Fowle in 1863 in the congressional chambers of the United State House of Representatives before four thousand guests.

Just after receiving their wedding guests, the Fowles went to the library they had worked so diligently to open in Washington, D.C., known as the Soldiers Free Library, for the benefit of Union soldiers. The Fowles had collected funds and books from numerous benefactors in the North. Among their friends was Eleanor Baker of Dorchester, who purchased fifty books herself and enlisted the aid of her friends in Dorchester. The Fowles provided a place for soldiers on leave to find quiet, with stationery, pens and stamps to write letters to loved ones at home. Books, tracts and scrapbooks were among the literature available, and occasionally an impromptu concert filled the library with song. The Fowles built the library from a small collection into one of renown and asked each soldier using the collection to sign a pledge to abstain from "profane language, from alcoholic drink, as a beverage, and from all other vices in the Army and Camp." Their departure from Washington, D.C., in 1863 prompted a resolution to thank the couple for their work in Washington; a Bible and photograph album were presented to them by their friends.

After the Civil War, the Fowles went to Brooklyn, New York, where John A. Fowle was in the wool brokerage trade. They remained there until 1877, when they moved to Dorchester, Massachusetts. They purchased a brick row house on Boston Street (now Columbia Road) across from the firehouse. In retirement, the couple remained active, with Mrs. Fowle founding the Wintergreen Club, a reading room in Upham's Corner for children. She founded the Grandchildren of the Veterans of the Civil War and became active in the Dorchester Historical Society, which was founded in 1891. Her husband wrote a short history of the Old North Burying Ground in Upham's Corner, across from their home, in 1912, and the two received greetings on their fiftieth wedding anniversary, which was celebrated in the Hall of Flags at the Massachusetts State House with over two thousand people in attendance. Their activities also included the raising of two daughters of Aunt Sally, a slave of Colonel Robert E. Lee. It was Aunt Sally who gave Mrs. Fowle a silver salver and a few pieces of china from Arlington House, the Lee home in Virginia, to keep for protection. A bond was developed between the two, and after the war the Fowles raised two of her children in the North, educating them there.

The Fowles' stories and experiences of the Civil War and their own participation in the events of that time attracted a plethora of friends. Their vast collection of Civil War relics was deposited at the Blake House in Dorchester. Upon her death in 1919, Elida was buried at Forest Hills Cemetery; Mrs. Fowle was the last remaining member of the Nurses of the Civil War. With her went many of the firsthand memories of a full and active life that revolved around the Civil War.

ELEANOR BAKER

Eleanor Jameson Williams Baker (1806–1891) was the second wife of Walter Baker and a well-known and beloved resident of Dorchester during the nineteenth century. Born in Boston on fashionable Fort Hill, she was the daughter of Robert Williams, a China trade merchant on Long Wharf in

Eleanor Jameson Williams Baker (1806–1891) was the second wife of Walter Baker, owner of the chocolate mill at Dorchester Lower Mills. A noted philanthropist, she supported many worthwhile causes and was said to have had "discriminating judgment and a boundless charity."

Boston. The Williamses were a well-to-do family, with Mr. Williams serving as a selectman of Boston and treasurer of the Society of the Cincinnati.

The Bakers were married in 1840 and lived first at 1126 Washington Street in Dorchester Lower Mills and then on Summer Street in the fashionable South End of Boston (now known as Downtown Crossing). Walter Baker later purchased the former Oliver estate on Washington Street, at the corner of Park Street (present site of the Lucy Stone School), as a summer house. The property was within driving distance of the mill on the Neponset River and afforded a secluded and panoramic home. The Bakers were the parents of four children, none of whom survived infancy. After the death, in 1852, of her husband, Mrs. Baker made her permanent home in Dorchester. She was a member of the Second Church of Dorchester at Codman Square, contributing large sums of money over the years. Her husband had donated the four-sided tower clock in 1852. It was in these years that she invited to her home world travelers, well-known guests and cultivated personages. In an undated newspaper clipping, it was said that Mrs. Baker "drew to herself a large number of friends in such a hospitable manner that she was never at a loss for companions all the rest of her life." It was commented in her obituary that "she had a strong character, an independent mind, a discriminating judgment and a boundless charity." Indeed, after her husband's death, she was more than comfortable in her circumstances and began to devote a great deal of time and money to worthy charities.

When the Civil War broke out, Mrs. Baker opened her home to Dorchester women, providing large quantities of linens and cotton material to supply the army hospitals. Donating a century-old dining tablecloth for bandages, she also gave freely of her fortune. She singlehandedly headed the Dorchester women who gathered numerous books and pamphlets for the Soldiers Free Library, a new establishment in Washington, D.C., opened by Elida Rumsey and John A. Fowle. Her wealth also allowed her to travel extensively when it was not a common occurrence to cross the Atlantic Ocean. She was charitable to those who made her acquaintance in Europe. During one of her journeys in Europe, on her return from the Holy Land, she met Dr. Samuel Gridley Howe (of the Perkins Institute for the Blind) in Athens and assisted him and his daughter in distributing the garments collected in Boston among the Cretan refugees on the Island of Egena, at the center of the Saronikos Gulf. Indeed, she had a somewhat continental benevolence and traveled far from Dorchester when not doing good works locally.

The Baker House, originally built by Lieutenant Governor Oliver prior to the American Revolution, was a large and imposing Georgian mansion facing Washington Street, with incredible views from the rear of Dorchester Bay and the Harbor Islands. The grounds extended down the hill to what is now Dorchester Avenue and were extended tracts of open land. The house had once been owned by the Honorable Benjamin Hitchborn, who entertained Presidents Jefferson and Madison in his home and also allowed the Dorchester Academy to use one of the rooms for its first school. The house attracted rich and poor, old and young, and it seemed that the only prerequisite for an invitation from Mrs. Baker was a sensible wit and proper manners. When Eleanor Baker died in 1891, her estate was considerable, and she remembered many of her friends, her church and her numerous charities. The mansion became the Colonial Club of Dorchester, a quasi country club that remained until just before World War I, though most of the land had been sold for speculative purposes, with Regina Road, Tremlett and Waldeck Streets, Wellesley Park and Upland Avenue being laid out. Mrs. Baker was a true soldier in her extensive benevolent works.

EMILY FIFIELD

There is an elementary school on Dunbar Avenue in Dorchester that was named for Emily Fifield, a noted educator, advocate for manual training in the public schools and the second female member of the Boston School Committee. She was well known for her work in the Woman's Alliance of the First Parish Church, where she served as national recording secretary for three decades.

Emily Porter Fifield (1840–1913) was born in Weymouth, the daughter of Thomas Brastow and Emily Vining Porter. Married in 1858 to Dr.

Emily Porter Fifield (1840–1913) was the second female member of the Boston School Committee, serving from 1883 to 1902. Mrs. Fifield was a noted educator and strong advocate for manual training in the city's public schools. In 1918, the City of Boston built a school designed by Harrison H. Atwood on Dunbar Avenue in Dorchester and named it in her memory.

William Cranch Bond Fifield, she lived in Harrison Square for five decades, a neighborhood in Dorchester now referred to as Clam Point.

The Fifields purchased a ready-built house from John Robinson on Ashland Street, which had been developed following the opening of the Old Colony Railroad. As a teacher in the Sunday school of the First Parish in Dorchester, she was to be elected to the Boston School Committee in 1884 as the second woman ever elected to that position; her predecessor was Abby May, an early exponent of the equal suffrage movement. These two women were shortly joined by Mary P.T. Hemenway, a wealthy philanthropist and founder of the manual arts and domestic science classes in the Boston Public Schools. The introduction of sewing and cooking for girls and woodworking, sloyd and manual arts for boys prepared them for jobs following their education, for far fewer went on to college a century ago. A respected authority on public school matters, Mrs. Fifield had nationwide fame as an advocate of manual training. It was said that she "traveled widely, lecturing on manual training and educational matters, and was a prominent advocate of the more extended use of the city's school plant."

During her service on the Boston School Committee, Mrs. Fifield "adopted" the Mechanic Arts School (later known as Boston Technical High School) and chaired a subcommittee that was "largely instrumental in causing [the school's] marked success." At that time, Mechanic Arts was a major feeder of students to "Tech," as the Massachusetts Institute of Technology was known. Upon her husband's death in 1896, she donated the funds and furnishings for the Fifield Room in the Boston Medical Library in his memory and erected a memorial granite horse trough at Meeting House Hill; thereafter, she began to retire from her numerous committees.

She later moved to Morton Hill in Milton, where she had the noted architect Edwin J. Lewis Jr. design her house at 77 Morton Road on land she had purchased from Nathaniel Safford. Mrs. Fifield and her daughter and son-in-law, Mary Fifield and Henry King, moved into the house in 1911, laying out perennial gardens that were planted with cuttings and roots from friends' gardens. The Fifield-King House was to become known as Kingfield after 1913 in honor of Henry King's surname and the "field" of Fifield. Upon her death at Kingfield in 1913, Mrs. Fifield was eulogized as a generous, concerned citizen whose efforts for the Mariners' House in Boston's North End, the School for Feeble-Minded Youth in South Boston and the Independent Voters' League did not go unnoticed.

ANNA CLAPP HARRIS SMITH

Nearly everyone in Dorchester has heard of or used the services of the Animal Rescue League, but few of us realize that it was founded by a Dorchester woman. Anna Clapp Harris Smith (1843–1937) was born at 65 Pleasant Street at the foot of Jones Hill and lived there her entire life. She was the daughter of William and Anna Larkin Clapp Harris and the great-granddaughter of David Clapp. The young Anna Clapp Harris, imbued with family connections and born to a world of comfort, was christened at the First Parish Church. As a child, she was intelligent and developed both a flair for music and a deep abiding feeling for animals and nature. It was said

Anna Clapp Harris Smith (1843–1937) was the founder, in 1899, of the Animal Rescue League of Boston. She coined the phrase "Kindness Uplifts the World," which is still the motto of the Animal Rescue League.

that her father was a strict and religious man and that these values, instilled in his daughter, gave a deep spiritual devotion to her great cause of later years.

Anna Harris completed her education in Boston after attending Miss Pope's School on Meeting House Hill. She became an accomplished musician and taught music, giving informal recitals with her brother Samuel, who was a talented violinist. She also composed music for several songs. The Harris family was comfortable and well established, and they were among the leaders of local society. In 1884, Anna Harris married Huntington Smith of Boston; he was the editor of the *Boston Beacon*, later to become its owner and publisher. The Smiths lived in the Harris family home, which was built by David Clapp on the stone foundations of the Thomas Jones House, reputedly built in 1636. The Clapp family had purchased the original house from Jones's heirs and rebuilt it after a disastrous fire in 1804. The five-bay Federal house, while not pretentious, was surrounded by lands that were not just extensive but also valuable. The Smiths subdivided their estate over the years into house lots.

Undoubtedly, Anna Smith was a compassionate person and tried to do the right thing concerning animals. But according to her biography, she was deeply shocked when a neighbor told her that when her cat became too old to catch mice, she would have it taken to the woods and left there. This apparently fueled Smith's desire to form some sort of protective circle for animals. As a member of the First Parish Church's Benevolent Society, then headed by Emily Fifield, Smith visited the sick and the poor. Apart from the human misery that she was, she was overwhelmed by the conditions of animals in back alleys and beasts of burden on the main streets of Boston. This concern became a driving force for Smith and culminated in the incorporation of the Animal Rescue League of Boston on March 13, 1899. Smith coined the phrase "Kindness Uplifts the World," which is still the league's motto. Throughout her long life, she had a great concern for all animals that she was able to combine with practical means to reduce suffering. True, her wealth and position enabled her to devote her days to better the conditions of animals, but it was her never-ending sense of duty that sustained her when it became her life's work.

Today, the Animal Rescue League takes in stray animals, most of which it spays and neuters, and tries to find them homes. In addition, the statewide group runs educational programs that teach children how to properly care for animals and has work crews that will pick up dead animals or rescue those that are caught in trees.

ALICE STONE BLACKWELL

As the only child of such prominent parents as Lucy Stone and Henry Browne Blackwell, Alice Blackwell was raised not only with a social conscience but also with a remarkably mature attitude for one so young. In her book *Growing Up in Boston's Gilded Age: The Journal of Alice Stone Blackwell*, author Marlene Merrill creates an impression of Alice's life in Dorchester and Boston in the 1870s.

Alice Stone Blackwell (1858–1950) was raised on Boutwell Street on Pope's Hill in Dorchester, where her parents moved in 1868. Pope's Hill was open land prior to the annexation of Dorchester to Boston in 1870, with only the Pope, Train, Spaulding and Pratt families owning houses on the

Alice Stone Blackwell (1858–1950) graduated from the Chauncey Hall School and Boston University and, after her mother's death in 1893, assumed the editorship of the *Women's Journal*.

hill. Alice Blackwell attended the Harris School, which was at the corner of Victory Road and Train Street. While attending this school, she began keeping a journal, recording her impressions of life and her friendships and enemies, as well as the daily routine of her well-run household, where she made barley candy one day and walked to the Lower Mills the next day. The journal, written during her teenage years, could be a more personal rather than broadly interesting recording of one's life, but Marlene Merrill has not only edited it for content but has also provided footnotes for those of us who do not know where Harrison Square or Tenean Beach are located.

As an only child, Alice Blackwell was an independent person who traveled to Boston from the Pope's Hill Station on the Old Colony Railroad after school. She visited the Boston Public Library and the Boston Athenaeum, borrowing books that today we might find few adults, let alone children, reading. Her walks about Boston usually ended when she visited the Boston office of the *Women's Journal*, the newspaper her mother edited on Tremont Place in Boston. As editor, Lucy Stone was continuing the "firsts" she was so well known for. We can imagine how proud Alice Blackwell must have been of her mother, but we can also sense her self-consciousness, her shyness and her concerns in life by reading her journal.

Alice kept the journal during the years just after Dorchester was annexed to the city of Boston. Her family, a noted and well-educated group of people, included her aunts, sisters Dr. Elizabeth and Dr. Emily Blackwell, and the Reverend Antoinette Blackwell, who were amongst the most respected and forthright women in America. Her life in suburban Dorchester offered not only lasting friendships but also a nurturing aspect to her life, as her parents both traveled throughout the country lecturing on women's rights. Her education at the Chauncey Hall School in Copley Square, Boston, and later at Boston University, gave her not only the education but also the confidence she would need to become a leader in the issue of women's rights.

Assisting her mother in the publication of the *Women's Journal*, Alice Blackwell later became editor of the newspaper upon her mother's death in 1893. Her father continued to offer advice and direction to his daughter, but he was more involved in the development of Neponset in the 1885 to 1905 period, laying out Bowman Street and Blackwell Street in the great development of Dorchester. Upon his death in 1907, Alice offered her family's home to the Morgan Memorial for one dollar per year so inner-city children might visit the countryside, till the soil and breathe clean air. Alice

Seated on the steps of the house her parents bought in 1869 on Pope's Hill are Alice Stone Blackwell (right) and her nurse. Miss Blackwell's benevolent efforts on behalf of the less fortunate and persecuted lasted until her death.

Blackwell continued her quest for women's rights and lived to see women attain the right to vote. Her efforts on behalf of the less fortunate were tremendous, and at one time, unable to give money, she sold the Persian rugs from her home on Pope's Hill to benefit the Armenians, over a million of whom perished in genocide at the hands of the Turks during World War I.

The journal of Alice Stone Blackwell offers a glimpse into the youth of a girl who was destined to follow in the footsteps of her mother. Just before Lucy Stone's death, she said to her daughter, "Make the world be a better place." Not only did Alice follow her mother's direction but also her personal journal makes the wonderful world of Victorian Dorchester and Boston come to life through the written word.

JOSEPHINE PRESTON PEABODY

Josephine Preston Peabody (1874–1922) was one of the most talented poets to have lived in Dorchester. She was born in 1874 in New York, the daughter of Charles and Susan J. Morrill Peabody. When she was a child, her father died. The family then moved to the home of her maternal grandparents, Charles and Susan Jackson Morrill, on King Street, Dorchester.

Peabody entered the Harris School on Mill Street (now Victory Road), the school attended earlier by Alice Stone Blackwell, the daughter of the famous women's rights advocate Lucy Stone. In 1887, while a student at the Harris School, Peabody began to write lyrical poetry, a form she continued through her admission to Girls' Latin School in Boston. Her poetry was so well received that it was published in both the *Atlantic Monthly* and *Scribner's*. She became a voracious writer, penning a novel, a comedy and twenty-two poems that appeared in magazines. Her appetite for writing was insatiable, and recognition was forthcoming. In 1892, she left Girls' Latin School due to ill health, writing numerous short stories and poems, many of which were

Josephine Preston Peabody (1874–1922) was one of the most talented poets at the turn of the twentieth century. Said to be able to create the impression of realism by using the printed word, she said of her writing that she was "wildly happy while I am doing it, though it doesn't for a moment dull the longing after color, and shan't neither!"

published. However, it was in 1894, when she entered Radcliffe College as a special student, that her writing took on new meaning and acquired a luster of prose. Her writings seemed to flow forth in a steady and even-paced rhythm. After two years at Radcliffe, she left in 1896. She continued to write and published poems such as "Old Greek Folk Stories," "The Wayfarers," "Fortune and Men's Eyes" and "Marlowe" by 1901, in addition to dramas, novels and short stories.

In 1899, she left the Morrill home in Dorchester to live on Linnaean Street in Cambridge. Undoubtedly, this area, known as Avon Hill and laid out as a streetcar suburb for the newly affluent, gave new impetus to her writings. In fact, she had written, "When my father died, we left New York and came to Dorchester in Darkest Suburbs." Undoubtedly, Cambridge, with its proximity to both Harvard and Radcliffe, offered a more supportive and understanding environment than Dorchester. Her travels to Europe began after her move, and she spent many months traveling through England, Scotland, Holland and Belgium. In 1901, she began a lecture position at Wellesley College that lasted two years. It was in 1906, however, that her life changed when she married Lionel S. Marks, professor of mechanical engineering at Harvard University.

The support of a husband allowed Josephine Peabody the luxury of the written word. She entered and won, over three hundred other participants, the Stratford Competition in England. Her play *The Piper* was thought to be so well written and enjoyable that she received much attention at its premiere in England. It was after her marriage that her writings, primarily published by Houghton-Mifflin, continued on: *The Singing Man* in 1911, the comedy *The Wolf of Gubbio* in 1913, *Harvest Moon* in 1916 and the play *Portrait of Mrs. W* in 1922.

Peabody's writings, so extensive for one so young, came to an end all too quickly when she died in 1922. Her reading public, probably unaware of her youth, was enthralled by her work. Peabody was able to create the impression of realism using the printed word. She once wrote: "I am wildly happy while I am doing it, though it doesn't for a moment dull the longing after color, and shan't neither!" No, the writing shan't dull, nor even lose its color, for as long as *The Book of the Little Past* exists, we can retreat into the world illuminated by Josephine Preston Peabody.

ROSE FITZGERALD KENNEDY

Rose Fitzgerald Kennedy (1890–1995) elicited not only the respect of this country but also our sympathy as the mother of four children who died in tragic circumstances. However, for all of the sorrow and grief in her life, and "control of her emotions for which a nation later held her in awe," Mrs. Kennedy maintained a sense of duty to her family and to the myriad charities she supported throughout her life.

Born in Boston's North End, Rose Fitzgerald was the daughter of John and Mary Hannon Fitzgerald. Her father, the son of Irish immigrants, campaigned for the position of mayor of Boston in 1905 against James Jackson Storrow, a wealthy Brahmin for whom Storrow Drive was named. Fitzgerald, with little financial support behind him, used the campaign slogan "Manhood against Money," which he hoped would equalize the campaign and thereby win him the support of the burgeoning immigrant community. After singing his trademark song "Sweet Adeline" to supporters at Faneuil Hall following a campaign speech, women were said to have swooned, and he was thereafter affectionately nicknamed "Honey Fitz," a moniker that was to remain with him throughout his political career.

The Fitzgeralds, after Honey Fitz was elected mayor of Boston, moved to a large Italianate mansion at the corner of Welles Avenue and Harley Street on Ashmont Hill in Dorchester. The house was built just prior to the annexation of Dorchester to Boston in 1870 and was, according to Rose Fitzgerald Kennedy, where they "lived in Dorchester very comfortably and happily for a good many years." Rose attended the nearby Dorchester High School in Codman Square, where she graduated with honors in 1905, her diploma being presented to her by her mayoral father. She had wanted to attend Wellesley College, but her father, on the advice of William Cardinal O'Connell, refused to allow her to go there, as it was a secular school. Instead, she attended the Convent of the Sacred Heart in Boston's Back Bay for a year before enrolling at Blumenthal in Holland. Her studies abroad allowed her not just the opportunity for just studies but also exposure to foreign students and cities.

Rose Fitzgerald returned to Dorchester in 1909, after her father was elected to a second term as mayor. The house on Welles Avenue, though large in scale, was the home to numerous brothers and sisters. Her debut in 1911 was held in the parlor at the family home and was attended by

The debut of Rose Fitzgerald (1890–1995) was held in 1911 at her parents' house on Welles Avenue on Ashmont Hill, Dorchester, with over four hundred guests attending. She and her mother, Mary Hannon Fitzgerald, received their guests in a parlor bedecked with roses and ferns.

approximately four hundred guests; the debutante's "frank, smiling face bade them welcome before they had hardly crossed the threshold." Receiving in front of a rose- and fern-bedecked parlor with her mother and her friends Miss Marguerite O'Callaghan, Miss Molly Welch and Miss Mary O'Connell, Rose "never lost her self possession…and had pleasant words for all." She said in her autobiography, *Times to Remember*, that her "debut was not lavish, at least by the standards of those times," but with the house decorated with southern smilax and orchids, and the large hall decorated with mountain laurel, it is hard to imagine such an event as not lavish. Numerous family and friends cabled their congratulations to Miss Fitzgerald, among them Sir Thomas Lipton of England, who said: "I extend my heartiest congratulations to you on the occasion of your coming out. I suppose that in a short time I will be sending congratulations for another occasion of great joy, that of your marriage."

Joseph Patrick Kennedy and Rose Elizabeth Fitzgerald were married on October 7, 1914, in a small ceremony at the private chapel at the residence of William Cardinal O'Connell in Boston.

In 1914, Rose married Joseph P. Kennedy, son of Patrick and Mary Hickey Kennedy of East Boston. He had attended Harvard University, and after their marriage by William Cardinal O'Connell in his private chapel at his residence, the newlyweds spent their honeymoon at the Greenbrier in White Sulpher Springs, West Virginia. After returning to Boston, they purchased a house at 83 Beals Street in Brookline, which is now a historic site open to the public. Much in the same vein as Rose's father, during his lifetime Joseph Kennedy was to become a successful banker, businessman and government servant. Throughout their life together, the Kennedys had a sense of commitment to both the public and to themselves. After business took them to Bronxville, New York, to live, Mrs. Kennedy still returned to St. Margaret's Hospital on Jones Hill in Dorchester for the birth of Jean and Edward Kennedy. Their interest in St. Margaret's Hospital was not just as a maternity hospital, where one of every two births in Boston occurred in the years prior to the 1960s, but also because it served a very necessary need for the community. The Sisters of Charity of St. Vincent de Paul offered services for unwed mothers, the immigrant community and the poverty of the inner city.

When President Franklin Delano Roosevelt appointed Joseph Kennedy ambassador to the court of Saint James, his family left for London, where they experienced much of the anxiety and concern that led up to the beginning of World War II. Mrs. Kennedy, for her good work and devotion to her faith, was made a papal countess by Pope Pius XII in 1951 for her exemplary charitable work. This work continued unabated for a further two decades, at which time she devoted her energies towards the mentally challenged. Her Flame of Hope project was said to have brought more understanding and financial support for those whose children were mentally handicapped. Her own daughter Rosemary's mental retardation spearheaded her work with the continued support of St. Coletta School (now Cardinal Cushing Centers) and the Joseph P. Kennedy Jr. Hospital in Brighton.

Her devotion to good works earned her many awards and recognitions in this country and abroad, but it was probably the lessons she learned on her father's knee on Welles Avenue on Ashmont Hill in Dorchester that served her through her lifetime. Her friendship with Richard Cardinal Cushing ensured her generosity to the archdiocese of Boston and continued her philanthropy for the schools and hospitals of the Roman Catholic Church. She set an example to which few of us can compare our commitments, with dedication and determination that made our community, and our country, a better place.

5

FELLOW TOWNSMEN
OF DORCHESTER

GOVERNOR WILLIAM STOUGHTON

William Stoughton (1631–1701) is often referred to as the last of the Puritans. Son of Israel and Elizabeth Knight Stoughton, he was born in England, and the family immigrated to Dorchester in the Massachusetts Bay Colony. His father was the owner of extensive landholdings in the Massachusetts Bay Colony and was granted permission by the Great and General Court to erect the first gristmill in New England on the Neponset River at Lower Mills. William Stoughton was educated at the Dorchester school and in 1650 graduated from Harvard College with a degree in theology. He continued his studies at New College, Oxford, graduating with a BA in theology in 1652 and a master's degree a year later. He served as a curate in Sussex, but as he was a Puritan minister serving during the Restoration of Charles II, he lost his position and returned to Massachusetts in 1662.

Stoughton and his family had a large income from the gristmill on the Neponset River and from their extensive landholdings throughout the colony, so he was able to pursue a career in public service. According to a biography of Increase Mather, Stoughton was thought by his seventeenth-century contemporaries to be "a person of eminent qualifications, honorable extract, liberal education, and singular piety." As the ambassador from the province of Massachusetts to the court of Britain, he was thought very capable. As chief justice of the superior court, he was well chosen, and he was nominated and elected lieutenant governor under Richard, Earl of Belmont, and governor of Massachusetts.

Governor William Stoughton (1631–1701) was often said to be the last of the Puritans due to his stern, narrow and unwavering countenance. He served as chief justice at the Salem witchcraft trials and as governor of the province of Massachusetts Bay from 1694 to 1699 and again in 1700 and 1701.

In 1689, after the "Glorious Revolution" in England, Belmont was succeeded by Sir William Phipps, although Stoughton, as lieutenant governor, had served as acting governor for a time.

Stoughton served as chief justice of the Special Court of Oyer and Terminer in 1692 and then as chief justice of the Superior Court of Judicature in 1693. It was during this time that Stoughton was appointed chief justice of the Salem witch trials. Witchcraft was a very real belief in the seventeenth century; unexplained occurrences and mysterious aspects of life frightened the stern Puritans. With the advent of accusations of sorcery in Salem Village in 1692, Governor Phipps promptly established a court to try the accused. This court, headed by William Stoughton, also included Judges Hathorne, Sewell and Curwin. Within a fortnight, the court found Bridget Bishop guilty of witchcraft, and she was hanged. A total of twenty-one "witches"—including two men—were either hanged or pressed to death by stones for their supposed crimes. The trials created fervor, and an anxious colony ultimately put a stop to them. Over time, the other three judges all publically repented in front of the congregations of their meetinghouses, asking for forgiveness. Only Stoughton refused to repent of his dark part as judge in the Salem witchcraft tragedy.

William Stoughton was "a Puritan, and, at times, was marked by a stern narrowness of thought by no means to his credit," according to his biographer. He was lauded for his capable demeanor and his ability, although many of those in Massachusetts held reservations. Nonetheless, according to the Reverend Increase Mather, son of Reverend Richard Mather of the Dorchester Meeting House, Stoughton was "not only a good Congregationalist, but a strong politician." Stoughton, who had never married, trained his nephew William Tailor in the public arena of the time. Stoughton served as acting governor of the province of Massachusetts Bay from 1694 to 1699 and as governor from 1700 to 1701, the year he died.

Governor Stoughton left a large legacy to Harvard College, which was used to build Stoughton Hall. He also bequeathed tracts of land in Dorchester to be leased for the support of Harvard College scholars and

The tomb of Governor William Stoughton is a large limestone monument in the Old North Burying Ground in Upham's Corner, Dorchester. The top was lettered in Latin and in 1828 was repaired by Harvard College, to which he bequeathed a large part of his fortune.

for the Dorchester school. He instructed that silver cups be made and engraved with the Stoughton crest and presented to both the Dorchester and Milton Meeting Houses. Stoughton left to his nephew William Tailor, son of William and Rebecca Stoughton Tailor, the family estate at the corner of Pleasant Street and Savin Hill Avenue, the gristmill on the Neponset River and an extensive portfolio of lands and investments that made him one of the wealthiest citizens of Massachusetts. William Tailor would later serve as governor of Massachusetts from 1715 to 1716 and again in 1730.

Both the Massachusetts town of Stoughton and the Dorchester street are named in honor of Governor William Stoughton. However, his dark involvement with the Salem witchcraft trials, so rarely mentioned, remains a blot on his otherwise impeccable record of public service. His tomb at the Old North Burying Ground at Upham's Corner has a large limestone crypt emblazoned with the Stoughton crest, testimony to the esteem in which he was held by his fellow Dorchesterites.

DR. JAMES BAKER

James Baker (1739–1825) was the son of James and Priscilla Paul Baker, who lived on the Upper Road (now Washington Street) at Melville Avenue in Dorchester, Massachusetts. He was educated at the North School. He graduated from Harvard College in 1760 and studied theology with the Reverend Jonathan Bowman (1703–1775), minister of the Dorchester Meeting House for forty-three years. Though he married Lydia Bowman (1741–1816), daughter of the Reverend Jonathan Bowman, he left his ministerial studies with her father and began the study of medicine. To support himself and his growing family, he taught school in Dorchester while studying medicine, but by 1762, he was keeping a general store at Baker's Corner (since 1848 known as Codman Square) at the present corner of Washington Street and Talbot Avenue.

In 1764, Dr. Baker, who would use his medical title for the remainder of his life, met and financially assisted John Hannon in setting up a chocolate mill in a rented mill on the Milton side of the Neponset River at Milton Village. Hannon was adept and skilled as a chocolate maker, having learned the trade in England. Backed by Baker, he produced "Hannon's

Dr. James Baker (1739–1825) was a graduate of Harvard College and, from 1765 to 1779, a financial backer of John Hannon, who produced "Hannon's Best Chocolate" at the Dorchester Lower Mills. In 1780, Dr. Baker founded the Baker Chocolate Company, which is today considered the oldest manufacturer of chocolate in this country.

Best Chocolate" from 1765 to 1779. In 1780, after Hannon disappeared on a supposed trip to the West Indies to procure cacao beans, Baker bought the interest from his widow, Elizabeth Gore Hannon, and commenced the manufacture of chocolate impressed with his own name.

Dr. Baker continued in the chocolate business, purchasing imported cacao beans from near and far, and was successful enough to build a fashionable house across from his old general store. The house, a five-bay Colonial, was elegantly furnished and included chairs made by Stephen Badlam, a well-known cabinetmaker in Dorchester Lower Mills. He and his wife, Lydia Bowman Baker, lived a comfortable life, thanks to the chocolate mill on the Neponset River, and in 1791, their son Edmund joined Baker in the chocolate business. In 1804, Dr. Baker retired from the business, and Edmund Baker assumed control.

THADDEUS MASON HARRIS, DD

Thaddeus Mason Harris, one of Dorchester's earliest historians, was the minister of the First Parish Church in Dorchester from 1793 to 1836. During his service to the town, his church underwent a great change when it split in a quandary over religious beliefs, and the Second Church in Codman Square was established in 1805. However, during the forty-three years he was minister on Meeting House Hill, Harris contributed greatly to both the spiritual and historical well-being of Dorchester.

Thaddeus Mason Harris (1768–1842) was born in Charlestown, the son of William and Rebekah Mason Harris. During the Revolution, the family moved to Choxet (now Lancaster) and remained there during the Siege

Reverend Thaddeus Mason Harris (1768–1842), minister of the First Parish in Dorchester from 1793 to 1836, was depicted by August Edouart in 1839 in a seated silhouette in Harris's library at Mount Ida in Dorchester. Harris was a classical scholar and a respected author of local history. *Author's collection.*

of Boston. His father died during the Revolution, and the Harris family lost their property in Charlestown, causing severe economic hardships. His mother encouraged him to become a maker of saddletrees. With the assistance of friends, Harris was able to enter Harvard College, graduating in 1787, after which he accepted a position as librarian at Harvard College from 1791 to 1793. It was during this time that he met, and then married, Mary Dix, aunt of the famous Dorothea L. Dix. Leaving his position, Harris studied and then prepared for the ministry under the guidance of Dr. Kendall of Weston, and he was called to the Dorchester Meeting House in 1793 after the Reverend Moses Everett died. Harris accepted the calling, and he became pastor of a church that could trace its founding to Plymouth, England, where the Puritans had established their church in 1630 before sailing on the *Mary and John* to the New World. He obviously had a sense of the history of his new church, and he lived up to the expectations of the congregation, serving until 1836.

The Harris family purchased a large tract of land on Bird's Hill, just west of Meeting House Hill. The land was hilly and had a panoramic

Mount Ida was built by Reverend Harris at the crest of Bird's Hill, just west of Meeting House Hill, where he preached for four decades. He cultivated the *Bon Chrétien* (Good Christian) pear on his estate, and the pear trees can be seen in the foreground.

view of Dorchester Bay. At the crest of the hill, Reverend Harris built a large mansion and named it Mount Ida. The estate comprised both gardens and pastureland and is today the area bounded by Bowdoin, Draper, Robinson and Adams Streets. The carriage drive to the mansion is now Mount Ida Road.

The devotion Reverend Harris showed to both his congregation and his town was unfailing, and he was widely respected by all who knew him. A classical scholar, speaking Greek and Latin, he was also a well-known writer. His book *A Chronological and Topographical Account of Dorchester* was printed in 1804 by the Massachusetts Historical Society. It recorded much early history of the town and described the ancient boundaries of Dorchester from the settlement of the town in 1630. His manuscript was long and detailed, and he said in his introduction:

> *Should it be thought that the narration is tediously minute, and incidents related which are quite trivial, I would observe that every particular in the early records of our history is important to the historian, and helps in delineating the features of its primitive character; whilst to the inhabitants of the town itself the more circumstantial the account, the more interesting and entertaining will it prove.*

Harris's writings, fascinating to historians, prove somewhat removed from general readers, but they offer up important and relevant trivia on the early town and its inhabitants. After Reverend Harris retired from the pulpit in 1839, he devoted the remainder of his life to historical research and writing at the library of the Massachusetts Historical Society, where he served as librarian, and at the Boston Athenaeum. He was so devoted and frequent a visitor to the Boston Athenaeum that after his death, in 1856, the noted author Nathaniel Hawthorne wrote to a friend in England of a meeting with a ghost in the reading rooms of that august library:

> *One of the worthies, whom I occasionally saw there was the Rev. Dr. Harris, a Unitarian clergyman of considerable repute and eminence…he resided, I think, at Dorchester, a suburban village in the immediate vicinity of Boston…I had never been personally acquainted with this good old clergyman, but had heard of him all my life as a noteworthy man…I remember it was on the street that I first noticed him. "Who is he" I inquired*

as soon as he had passed. "The Reverend Dr. Harris of Dorchester" replied my friend, and from that time I often saw him and never forgot his aspect…This reverend figure was accustomed to sit, day after day, in the self-same chair by the fireside; and by degrees, seeing him there constantly, I began to look toward him as I entered the reading room, and felt that kind of acquaintance at least on my part was established…One day especially (about noon, as was generally his hour) I am perfectly certain that I had seen this figure of Dr. Harris and had taken my customary note of him. But that very evening a friend said to me "Did you hear that old Dr. Harris is dead?" "No" said I, very quietly, "it cannot be true, for I saw him at the Athenaeum today." "You must be mistaken," rejoined my friend. "He is certainly dead," and confirmed the fact with such special circumstances I could no longer doubt it. The next day as I ascended the steps of the Athenaeum I remember thinking within myself, "Well I shall never see old Dr. Harris again." With this thought in my mind as I opened the door of the reading room, I glanced toward the spot and chair where Dr. Harris usually sat, and there to my astonishment sat the gray, infirm figure of the deceased Doctor reading the newspapers as was his wont. His own death must have been recorded, that very morning, in that very newspaper—From that time, for a long time thereafter, for weeks at least, and I know not but for months, I used to see the figure of Dr. Harris quite as frequently as before his death. It grew to be so common that at length I regarded the venerable defunct no more than any of the other old fogies who basked before the fire…To the best of my recollection I never observed the old gentleman either enter the reading room or depart from it or move his chair or lay down the newspaper or exchange a look with any person in the company, unless it were myself. He was not by any means invariably in his place. In the evening, for instance, though often at the reading room myself, I never saw him. It was at the brightest noontime I used to behold him, sitting within the most comfortable focus of the fire as real and lifelike an object (except he was so very old and of an ashen complexion) as any other in the room.

An apparition, or was it really the ghost of Thaddeus Mason Harris? Well, if there does prove to be an afterlife, it's comforting to know that historians' ghosts are still allowed to read in the Boston Athenaeum.

DANIEL DAVENPORT

The Old North Burying Ground in Upham's Corner is the oldest burial place in Dorchester, predating the South Burying Ground on Dorchester Avenue by almost two centuries. Since 1634, when it was laid out by a vote of the selectmen of Dorchester, it has been the resting place of many important residents, but none was more readily identifiable with the Old North in the nineteenth century than "Uncle" Daniel Davenport.

Daniel Davenport (1773–1860) was the son of Isaac and Mary Davenport of Dorchester. He was married to Sally Spur in 1796 by the Reverend Thaddeus Mason Harris, and they built a house in Cracker Hollow, the area off Geneva Avenue near Bowdoin Street, so named for the fact that crackers were baked in the vicinity. As a young man, Davenport succeeded Thomas Clap as sexton of the meetinghouse and also as the town gravedigger in 1799.

Daniel Davenport (1773–1860) was the sexton of the First Parish Church and the gravedigger at the Old North Burying Ground in Dorchester. He dug 730 of his fellow townsmen's graves for forty-nine years and then prepared his own years before it was actually needed.

The Old North Burying Ground, laid out in 1634 as a "five-rod-square enclosure," is an overlay of four centuries of Dorchester families who were interred in what was to become the "Garden of the Dead" in the mid-nineteenth century when Samuel Downer planted trees and flowering shrubs to create an arboretum cemetery.

Clap had served the town from 1760 to 1797 as sexton and gravedigger and had buried 1,080 of his fellow townsmen at Cemetery Corners, as Upham's Corner was known in the eighteenth century. Daniel Davenport, a father of numerous children and uncle of even more nephews and nieces, was beloved by many people. Among his duties as sexton was filling the foot warmers with hot coals on Sunday mornings to comfort those attending the long services in the unheated meetinghouse.

Davenport's interest in the Old North Burying Ground is evident in the publication of the *Sexton's Monitor, and Dorchester Cemetery Memorial*, printed in 1826.

Not only did he list interesting inscriptions on many of the tombstones at Old North, but he also included an important record of the ministers, ruling elders and deacons of Dorchester and a "Table of Annual Deaths" from the seventeenth century to 1825. Though it might not have been important when it was first published, this information is vastly important in the research of Dorchester's history today. Davenport must have realized that he was preserving some of Dorchester's history, for in this memorial he said, "When I read the several dates on the tombs, of some that died as yesterday, and some centuries ago, I consider that great day, when we shall all of us be contemporaries, and make our appearance together."

In 1833, after thirty-four years as the town gravedigger, Davenport must have felt his mortality, and he asked the Reverend Thaddeus Mason Harris to compose his tombstone epitaph:

> *This grave was dug and finished in the year 1833 by himself*
> *when he had been sexton 27 years and attended 1135 funerals.*
> *As Sexton with spade I learned to delve beneath the sod.*
> *Where body to Earth returns but Spirit to its God, years twenty seven this*
>   *toil I bore.*
> *And midst deaths of it was spared. Seven hundred graves and thirty I dug then*
>   *mine was prepared. And when at last I too must die.*
> *Some else the bed I must tole*
> *As here my Mortal relicks lie*
> *May Heaven receive my soul.*

His tombstone, a large slate stone, was carved and erected, but the grave remained empty until 1860, when "Uncle" Daniel Davenport died at the age of eighty-seven. His retirement, which had occurred in 1852, was a smooth transition for the town, as the new sexton and gravedigger was his son, William Davenport.

The Old North Burying Ground, which remained relatively neglected for two centuries, became a virtual garden in the mid-nineteenth century when Samuel Downer Sr., a noted horticulturalist and resident of Jones Hill, began to embellish the grounds with trees and flowering shrubs to emulate the new arboretum-inspired Mount Auburn Cemetery in Cambridge. The aspect of embellishing the Old North was an important one, and as the "resting place of our forefathers" it became, and still remains, a place of reverent reflection of the town, its history and of "Uncle" Daniel Davenport. Davenport said that "when I look upon the tombs of the great, every motion of envy dies within me" and that "when I meet with the grief of parents on a tombstone, my heart melts with compassion."

Daniel Davenport provided a necessary service to the town of Dorchester for decades, and he provided this service with respect and compassion. Let us recognize his contributions as important ones in Dorchester's "Garden of the Dead":

Come with me to the garden,
That sacred spot of earth,
Where ne'er is heard the airy song,
Nor the wonton sound of mirth.

CAPTAIN JOHN PERCIVAL

Captain John Percival (1779–1862) was an officer in the United States Navy during the War of 1812, the campaign against the West Indies pirates and the Mexican-American War. His daring, intense command style and sometimes legendary reputation led to him being affectionately called "Mad Jack" Percival.

Percival was born on Scorton Hill in the small village of West Barnstable on Cape Cod, and according to his headstone, he "left there at the age of 14 years," entering the navy as a cabin boy. He signed on as a ship's mate because there were few jobs that did not require lengthy apprenticeships. After a period of time, Percival joined the Merchant Marine service, only to be impressed on the British vessel HMS *Victory* under Lord Jarvis. This was a recurring problem for American sailors because an impressed sailor was rarely allowed to return to his native country. Percival managed, however, by placing a pistol at a sentry's head, thereby allowing him to escape to the American merchant ship *Washington*.

During the War of 1812, which was to engage Great Britain and the United States, Percival became sailing master of the *Peacock* and by a strange coincidence encountered the *Epervier* in a sea battle, capturing the ship. He was thereby promoted to lieutenant. The mariner's services during the war were invaluable to the American cause, and Percival was routinely promoted in a series of appointments that included line officer, lieutenant and then captain. So esteemed was his brave service to the country that the United States Congress presented him with a handsome sword. After the war, Percival was dispatched to the West Indies on the sloop *Cyane* to destroy the barbarous pirates who were committing indignities to those who crossed their paths. After a short period of time, Captain Percival's conquest of these infidels proved so effective that he broke and destroyed their forces.

Captain John Percival (1779–1862) was often referred to as "Mad Jack" Percival due to his daring and brave exploits in the United States Navy. He commanded the USS *Constitution* on the warship's only world circumnavigation between 1844 and 1846. Percival Street perpetuates his memory in Dorchester.

In 1841, his promotion to captain was instrumental in saving and restoring the USS *Constitution*; he sailed the famous warship around the world from 1844 to 1846, the ship's only circumnavigation. His long service to his country made him a legend. Nathaniel Hawthorne wrote of him and his daring exploits, and Herman Melville based a character on him in his novel *Moby Dick*. Percival retired to the small home he and his wife, Maria Pinkerton Percival (1793–1862), the daughter of David Smith Pinkerton of Trenton, New Jersey, had at the corner of Bowdoin and Percival Streets on Meeting House Hill in Dorchester. Captain Percival died at his home, which had originally been built by the Reverend Thaddeus Mason Harris for his son, William Mason Harris, in the early nineteenth century. Known as the Percival Cottage, it was moved back in 1872 to the slope behind the property when St. Peter's Church, designed by Patrick J. Keeley, was built on the site.

The cottage was remodeled as the rectory of the church, and there Father Peter Ronan, and his mother and sister, lived during his pastorate.

"Mad Jack" Percival was buried beside his wife at the West Barnstable Cemetery, in a lot overlooking Route 6A with identical granite headstones. He is a nationally important hero whose only remaining memorial in Dorchester is the street laid out adjacent to his cottage that bears his name.

ENOCH TRAIN

Train Street on Pope's Hill extends from Ashmont Street to Victory Road and has newer houses than most of Dorchester. The street was named for Colonel Enoch Train, a Boston merchant who lived at 88 Mount Vernon

Enoch Train (1801–1868) was founder of the White Diamond Line, which was in direct competition with the Cunard Line, both of which had ships sailing from Liverpool, England, to Boston. A well-respected and successful merchant, by the mid-nineteenth century he had further expanded his business to the Baltic and South America. Train Street perpetuates his memory in Dorchester.

Street on Boston's Beacon Hill and had a summer house on Pope's Hill. Enoch Train (1801–1868) was born in Weston. He became a merchant in Boston and in 1844 started the White Diamond Line, a shipping firm that ran clipper ships from Boston to Liverpool, England; its house flag was a white lozenge throughout a red field. Train's line was in direct competition with the Cunard Line, and within a few years, though initially viewed with skepticism, Train became a leading shipping merchant in Boston, with his business offices on Lewis Wharf. In the period prior to the Civil War, numerous Europeans were immigrating to this country, and the transatlantic shipping packets provided transportation to the New World. Train's ships were built by the renowned shipbuilder Donald McKay at his shipyards in East Boston and were among the swiftest crossing the Atlantic Ocean.

Within a few years of founding his line, Train had commissioned numerous clipper ships from McKay, who is thought to have been among the most capable shipbuilders in nineteenth-century America. The Train Line included the *Joshua Bates*, the *Washington Irving*, the *Anglo American*, the *Parliament*, the *Daniel Webster*, the *Staffordshire*, the *Chariot of Fame* and the *Star of Empire*, all of which were built at the McKay Shipyards and flew the distinctive red flag emblazoned with a white diamond. The foremast's sail had a large black "T," further signifying ownership by the Train Line. In the book *Recollections of Boston Merchants*, Aaron Sargent describes Enoch Train as "tall and erect with [a] manly step." In 1855, in partnership with George Upton, Donald McKay, Andrew Hall and James Bebee, Train started the Boston & European Steamship Company. Train expanded his Boston to Liverpool run with shipping to the Baltic, as well as South America. Clipper ships began to give way to steamships, which crossed the Atlantic Ocean quicker and with more comfort for passengers. This advanced approach to steamships led to many of the ships of the late nineteenth and early twentieth centuries.

Enoch Train was a public-spirited man, and in 1855, according to William Dana Orcutt's *Good Old Dorchester*, he "was one of a committee to host Edward Everett to speak in Dorchester upon the Eightieth Anniversary of the Evacuation of Boston." This public oration was given at Meeting House Hill, and Everett delivered a powerful speech befitting his position as the premier orator of his day. Train had married Adeline Dutton, the daughter of Silas and Nancy Tobey Dutton. Their only daughter was Adeline Dutton Train Whitney, wife of Seth Dunbar Whitney of Milton, who wrote numerous books throughout the late nineteenth century.

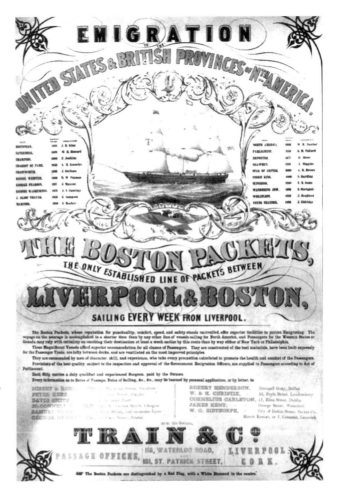

The Train Line connected Liverpool and Boston, with a weekly sailing in the mid-nineteenth century. The line, in direct competition with the Cunard Line of Sir Samuel Cunard, offered "Emigration to the United States and British Provinces in North America" on clipper ships built by Donald McKay of East Boston.

Though Enoch Train died in 1868, two years before Dorchester was annexed to the city of Boston, he was an early advocate for the annexation. His estate included vast tracts of land in Dorchester, with a street on the slope of Pope's Hill perpetuating his memory.

NAHUM CAPEN

The Ronan Park area on Meeting House Hill has one of the most panoramic views of Boston Harbor from any vantage point in Dorchester. A century ago, the park and the surrounding residential streets were once part of

Mount Ida, the estate of Nahum Capen, a publisher, writer and "tireless student of natural science and politics."

Since before the American Revolution, Meeting House Hill was a respectable area for homes, and it was on the summit of Bird's Hill, as it was then known, that the Reverend Thaddeus Mason Harris, minister of the First Parish Church, built his Federal-style mansion in the late eighteenth century. He named his estate Mount Ida, now the name of a street lined with three-deckers carved out of what was once Harris's estate. A well-to-do minister, Harris wrote extensively on both local and regional history. One wonders if his writings were influenced by the panoramic scenery from his study window. After his death in 1842, the estate was purchased by Nahum Capen, a prominent writer, bookseller and publisher in Boston.

Nahum Capen (1804–1886) had "an active mind, was fond of books, and...[was] to cultivate the art of expression." Widely known as an author and publisher, he rewrote *Plutarch's Lives*, adding notes and comments. He introduced the corner mailbox, at his own expense, while serving as postmaster of Boston and also instituted free delivery service of mail to residences in Boston.

Nahum Capen (1804–1886) was born in Canton, a town formerly a part of Dorchester. He was a partner in the firm of Marsh, Capen and Lyon, a prominent publishing company in Boston, and published the first volume of Edgar Allen Poe's works. Capen was a noted author and wrote *The History of Man* and *The History of Democracy*, in addition to numerous other books and pamphlets. He was appointed postmaster general of Boston, a position he held from 1857 to 1861. Capen instituted the collection of mail from iron boxes placed at strategic locations throughout Boston proper. To get the program started, and generally accepted by the public, he paid for these mailboxes, said to be the first in United States history, out of his own pocket. The new mail system worked so well that the corner mailbox survives to this day. Also while postmaster, Capen began the free delivery service of mail to residential homes, a first for Boston, as well as to stations of delivery in large cities. Before his term as postmaster general, one had to pick up mail at the post office.

When Capen and his family first purchased Mount Ida from the Harris family, they made few changes to the house, which stood where the Ronan

The Capen House, built by Reverend Harris, commanded the crest of Bird's Hill with panoramic views of Dorchester and the harbor. Today, the site of the estate is Ronan Park, designed by G. Henri Desmond of Desmond & Lord and named for Father Peter Ronan (1842–1917), first pastor of St. Peter's Church in Dorchester.

Park playground is today. However, at great expense, he added scenic wallpaper by Zuber, which came in polychromatic colors depicting the Boston Tea Party and imaginary scenes; certain colors were even painted in on site. The house was a well-kept mansion, filled with rare works of art and collections brought back to Dorchester by the Capens on their travels abroad. Roughly speaking, the estate was bounded by what are now Bowdoin, Percival, Robinson and Norton Streets, today the home of many Dorchesterites.

After the city of Boston annexed Dorchester in 1870, the Capens began to subdivide their estate. In 1872, they sold a portion of the estate to the Roman Catholic Archdiocese of Boston for the building of St. Peter's Church and its rectory and convent along Bowdoin Street. The puddingstone used to build the church was quarried from the rock ledge at the corner of the estate. As it was cut, Nahum Capen allowed the builders to store the pieces on his property until used. In 1899, the family sold nine acres of additional land

Edward Nahum Capen (1838–1915) lived most of his life at Mount Ida. He was a partner in the Boston oil concern of Capen & Pierce but was eventually associated with the Standard Oil Company for thirty years. Abbie Farwell Brown eulogized him as a "good citizen, loyal associate, kind friend, generous home-maker, in every relation of life he endeared himself to all."

through a syndicate, and Mount Ida Road, Draper Street, Hamilton Street and others were cut through the old estate. These new residential blocks were largely developed during the first two decades of the twentieth century. Still commanding a seat of prominence, the house remained virtually untouched until the death, in 1915, of Edward Nahum Capen, Nahum Capen's son. Edward was the sole remaining Capen family member at Mount Ida, and his death prompted local antiquarian Mary Fifield King to remark, "My how fast Dorchester changes."

Yes, the Dorchester known to those prior to the annexation saw tremendous changes, from the streetcars put through on Bowdoin Street to the building of St. Peter's Roman Catholic Church on the edge of what had been the estate of the minister of the First Parish Church. And then the last great estate house, Capen's Mount Ida, was demolished in 1916. Dorchester had changed fast. After Edward Nahum Capen's death, the estate was subdivided for both development and a public park, designed by G. Henri Desmond of Desmond & Lord and named in honor of Reverend Peter Ronan (1842–1917), pastor of St. Peter's Church. The remaining land was sold off, with the new three-deckers along Mount Ida Road having superb views of the bay. The famous wallpaper is almost all that remains of the former estate. The thick paper was removed from the walls in 1915 and rehung at a niece's summer house in Camden, Maine. The pergola and garden ornaments were also saved, and they represent some of the last few relics to trace a once-famous Dorchester landmark and the former home of the man who created the corner mailbox.

SAMUEL STILLMAN PIERCE

S.S. Pierce & Company brings to mind to most of us neatly packaged foodstuffs that arrive by mail—or earlier, by deliveryman—in red boxes with the distinctive crest of the firm emblazoned on the wrappings. The company stood for gourmet foods and exotic imports, such as reindeer tongue, which was largely unavailable in Dorchester a century ago.

Samuel Stillman Pierce (1807–1880) was born on Adams Street in the Cedar Grove neighborhood of Dorchester. The Pierce family had settled in Dorchester shortly after the town was settled in 1630 and descended from Robert and Anne Greenway Pierce, who built their house in the mid-

Samuel Stillman Pierce (1807–1881) was a purveyor of fancy groceries and wines to generations of discriminating Bostonians. His firm was known as S.S. Pierce & Company and was started in 1831 at the corner of Tremont and Court Streets in Boston. Red boxes emblazoned with the distinctive crest of the company were delivered near and far.

seventeenth century on what is today Oakton Avenue. The house, which still stands and is preserved by Historic New England, is a fine example of East Anglican architecture and was one of the few houses in southern Dorchester in the years prior to the Revolution.

Samuel S. Pierce was the son of Daniel and Lydia Davenport Pierce and was born in the farmhouse built by his family in the mid-eighteenth century. Daniel Pierce was a cabinetmaker, and though we know of no ascribed furniture, the proximity of his home to the Lower Mills, a veritable beehive of artisans and cabinetmakers, may have resulted in his craft being undertaken at home. His son Samuel, however, was apprenticed to a firm of importers in Boston and then went into the grocery business while still a young man. In 1831, Pierce founded his own grocery store and commenced a business that catered to families in Boston, with expert care and attention paid not just to the quality of the produce and provisions he offered but also to the presentation of the product and the maintenance of satisfied customers.

The first store of S.S. Pierce & Company was at the corner of Tremont and Court Streets in Boston, in a large granite building that housed his grocery store on the first floor and offices above. The store stocked thousands of items, many of which had limited sale to the general public. Requests in the years prior to the Civil War for kangaroo tail soup, truffled lark and reindeer tongue were made by Bostonians, according to C. Lester Walker, who wrote an article for *Reader's Digest*. According to the article, the store might annually sell "5,000 tureens of pate de fois gras, 45,000 jars of caviar and 95,000 cans of mushrooms"; it also sold "crepe suzette, English lime marmalade, French frogs legs and costly terrapin stew...the firm even stocks escargots and boxes of pink French snail shells to cook them in." Needless to say, one wonders how Bostonians had become so cosmopolitan with their refined palates over a century and a half ago.

The Pierce summer house was on Marsh Street (now Gallivan Boulevard) in Dorchester. After the death, in 1920, of Henrietta Pierce, the land was sold to the Archdiocese of Boston, and St. Brendan's Church was built facing Gallivan Boulevard. The remaining estate was subdivided for new streets such as Lennoxdale, Myrtlebank, Rockne and Crockett Streets and St. Brendan's Road.

S.S. Pierce was an astute businessman, and his large family provided four generations of Pierces to maintain both the name and the high standards of excellence that S.S. Pierce & Company had become known to represent. The diversity, quality and rareness of the foods offered by Pierce were unexcelled, and

> *some Bostonians claim that S.S. Pierce has introduced more new food products to Americans than any other U.S. grocer. The first recorded sale of canned corn was made by Samuel Pierce in 1848. Pierce's sold Singapore pineapple before Hawaiian was ever heard of. And sun-ripened canned peaches, brook trout from Iceland, even rattlesnake meat.*

Needless to say, Pierce maintained a business without rival and was not simply a self-made man but also an astute judge of Bostonians and their desire for gourmet and luxury foods. He sold liquor while most Bostonians ascribed to the Total Abstinence Pledge, in which one pledged never to indulge in "evil spirits." S.S. Pierce included "Twice Across Madeira" wine in his shop with the assurance that it was "shipped from Funchal, Madeira to New York, transshipped to Buenos Aires and then back to New York, thus having twice crossed the Equator." The Madeira was surely of fine quality, but the cachet was to make this particular brand of Madeira one of the bestsellers in New England.

With the finest foods available at this Boston store, imported Madeira and wines from Europe and a supportive customer base that patronized his business, Pierce purchased a large row house on Union Park in Boston's newly fashionable South End. His family—his wife, Ellen Maria Theresa Wallis, whom he married in 1836, and eight children—lived in Boston during the winters and summered at a house he owned in Dorchester. The house, enlarged after the Civil War to accommodate his family, stood on a knoll overlooking Sunnyside, the area of Adams Village today, and the Neponset River. The estate comprised a house and stable, with ten acres and marshland. Though S.S. Pierce died in 1880, his son Wallis Lincoln Pierce continued the trademark name and standards established by his father. The family—among them Samuel S. Pierce Jr., who died as a young man in California; Dr. M. Vassar Pierce, a noted Milton physician; and Holden White Pierce—maintained their connection to Dorchester, as their sister Henrietta still summered in the family home. The Pierce summer house, by the time of World War I, was a rambling series of additions made over the years. With dormers, ells and outbuildings, one can imagine the activity of the family during the summer in Dorchester.

However, times were changing, and along Minot Street, just north of the estate, three-deckers were being built on former farmland. Miss Pierce died in 1920, and her heirs sold a portion of the property to the Archdiocese of Boston; shortly thereafter, St. Brendan's Church was built facing the new Gallivan Boulevard. The laying out of Lennoxdale, Myrtlebank, Rockne and Crockett Streets and St. Brendan's Road was to take the remaining portion of the Pierce estate and allow for the building of the houses that represent one of the most charming neighborhoods on the site of the Pierce summer house.

S.S. Pierce & Company was founded in Boston but by a Dorchesterite, born and bred. The sense of both quality and luxury has been ever present in the foods offered by the firm, and the company boasts an unsurpassable ability to please, in every sense of the word. The firm still exists, in a reduced capacity, but still provides quality foods for institutions and schools. With the same crest emblazoned on its canned food, we realize that with over a century and a half of service to New England, Samuel S. Pierce is remembered, and his accomplishments are shared, with pride.

COLONEL CHARLES BARNARD FOX

With the sensationalism garnered in the movie *Glory*, we reveled in the drama and impact of the Civil War; however, the film also served to remind us of why that war was fought. The Fifty-fourth Regiment, led by Colonel Robert Gould Shaw, was the first African American regiment formed in Massachusetts, yet few of us realize that the Fifty-fifth Regiment, the second African American regiment, was led by a Dorchester resident. Charles Barnard Fox (1833–1895) was the son of the Reverend Thomas B. Fox, editor of the *Boston Transcript*. He was born in Newburyport while his father was minister of the Unitarian church in that town, but the family moved to Dorchester in 1845. Educated in the local schools, Fox entered the field of civil engineering. His brother, the noted architect John A. Fox, was also a civil engineer and is considered the father of Stick-style architecture in this country.

Colonel Charles Barnard Fox (1833–1895) led the Fifty-fifth Regiment, an African American Civil War troop that was trained at Camp Meigs. Fox had a "high standard of what a regiment should be." He was a partner in Holbrook & Fox, a leading real estate and land auction house in Boston. *Courtesy of John B. Fox.*

Fox had enlisted in the Civil War at Lyceum Hall on Meeting House Hill, the local recruiting office. With his brothers, John A. Fox and Thomas B. Fox Jr., he was encouraged to enlist by his maternal grandmother, Lucy Tappan Pierce, who came from an ardently abolitionist family. He received his commission as second lieutenant in the Thirteenth Massachusetts Infantry; one year later, he was made first lieutenant. In 1863, he was transferred to the Second Massachusetts Cavalry with the same rank. That same year, he was made major of the African American Fifty-fifth Regiment and was promoted to the rank of lieutenant colonel on November 3, 1863. The Fifty-fifth Regiment had been trained at Camp Meigs and was composed of men who had everything at stake in the war. Fox and his fellow officers were well trained and commended for their service, and it was said that Fox "had a high standard of what a regiment should be, and he endeavored to bring his men up to it." Fox's obituary read, in part:

> *It was abundantly shown in his long and meritorious service in the army during the civil war, and especially in his readiness to enter a branch of the service that was not regarded with favor even by many who in theory favored perfect equality between races, and which was not calculated to attract the young soldier powerfully, in comparison with the more popular and agreeable positions in white regiments. But Colonel Fox believed in the equality of the black men with the white, and whatever he believed he lived up to, and the relations which existed between him and the colored soldiers in his command were ever the most intimate and mutually regardful nature.*

Fox was reared in the Unitarian faith, and upon the family's removal in 1845 to Dorchester, they became connected with the First Parish Church on Meeting House Hill. The minister was the Reverend Nathaniel Hall, a fierce antislavery opponent who expounded on the evils of both slavery and the subjugation of African Americans in the South. His sermons, many of which were published for a more general readership, were vociferous and pointed to his belief that slavery was immoral and could only be abolished through the war. Charles B. Fox was undoubtedly influenced by Hall, and by his own father's opinion, which was quite often read in the daily editions of the *Boston Transcript*.

Charles Barnard Fox served in the Army of the Potomac until after the Battle of Fredericksburg, in the Siege of Charleston and in the Campaign in Florida, the Battle of Honey Hill being particularly gruesome. His record of bravery and courage was made known when he was made brevet colonel of the Fifty-fifth Regiment; he resigned his commission on June 25, 1865, at the end of the Civil War and decided to remain in the South. For three years after the war, Fox managed a cotton plantation on Sea Island off the coast of South Carolina. It was not until 1868 that he returned to Boston, becoming an inspector at the Boston Custom House. In partnership with his brother and his friends, he assisted in the establishment of Holbrook & Fox, a real estate and land auction house in Boston. It was his friend Silas Pinckney Holbrook and his brother John Andrews Fox who created the partnership. The firm of Holbrook & Fox was one of the leading firms of its kind in New England and was well respected for the development of the real estate market in the late nineteenth century. Colonel Thomas and Ruth Prouty Fox built their home, designed by his architect brother, on Fuller Street in Dorchester. His connection with the development of the old farms and estates of Dorchester continued until his untimely death in 1895.

The contributions of Colonel Charles Barnard Fox in regards to the Civil War were important enough to have his convictions and personal beliefs supersede his comfort. He served the members of the Fifty-fifth Regiment well and earned their respect with the title of colonel by brevet, an honor that few officers received for their service in the Civil War.

HENRY LILLIE PIERCE

In 1896, the city of Boston named the intersection of Dorchester Avenue and Washington and Adams Streets in Dorchester Lower Mills Pierce Square in memory of Henry Lillie Pierce. Today, few residents realize that this is the official name of the Lower Mills intersection; neither are they familiar with the myriad accomplishments of the man for whom it was named.

Henry Lillie Pierce (1825–1896) was the son of Colonel Jesse Pierce (1788–1856) and Elizabeth Vose Lillie Pierce (1786–1871) of Stoughton, Massachusetts. His father had been an educator at Milton Academy and later served in the Massachusetts House of Representatives. As a gentleman farmer, he maintained a large farm in Stoughton (formerly a part of Dorchester) until he moved, in 1849, to Washington Street in the Lower Mills of Dorchester with his wife and two sons. Edward Lillie Pierce was then attending Brown University, while Henry Lillie Pierce was at Milton Academy and was to later attend the Bridgewater Normal School.

In 1849, Henry L. Pierce was hired to work as a clerk at the Baker Chocolate Company. Walter Baker, the owner of the chocolate company and stepbrother of Pierce's mother, hired him at a salary of three dollars per week. However, as their political views invariably clashed and caused tremendous animosity (Pierce was a vociferous and deeply opinionated Free-Soiler), Pierce left after only a year of politically tinged employment to take up newspaper work in the Midwest. At the request of Sydney Williams, brother-in-law of Baker and managing director of the chocolate mill, Pierce

Henry Lillie Pierce (1825–1896) increased the Baker Chocolate Company fortyfold while he was president between 1854 and 1896. He was to build numerous mills, increase the workforce and adopt La Belle Chocolatière as the registered trademark of his sweet chocolate empire.

returned to Boston after a year and was appointed manager of the Walter Baker Counting House at 32 South Market Street in Boston (now a part of the Quincy Market retail area). Pierce was obviously a hard worker, for after the deaths of both Walter Baker (in 1852) and Sydney Williams (in 1854), he was permitted to lease the chocolate business from the trustees of the Baker estate. The trustees of the Baker estate, fully aware that Pierce had only been with the company for five years, leased the business to him for a two-year probationary period, "subject to a life interest payable annually to Mrs. Baker," widow of the late owner and step-aunt to Pierce, until her death in 1891. He began manufacturing under the name and style of Walter Baker & Company. He was obviously successful, for in 1856 the trustees extended the lease another eight years, during which time Pierce began an expansion that would eventually absorb his competitive chocolate manufacturers in the Lower Mills. The trustees continued the ten-year lease until 1884, when "all terms under the Walter Baker will having been satisfied, the entire property is conveyed by the Trustees to Henry L. Pierce."

In 1897, the junction of Dorchester Avenue and Washington and Adams Streets was named Pierce Square in memory of Henry L. Pierce, owner of the Baker Chocolate Company and mayor of Boston in 1872 and 1877.

In 1860, Pierce bought the Preston Chocolate Mill from Henry D. Chapin, to whom it had been sold the previous year, and in 1881, Josiah Webb sold his chocolate mill to Pierce. In 1864, the trustees of the Baker estate renewed the lease for a second decade. This decade was decisive for Pierce, as he began to enter his chocolate in competitive exhibitions both in this country and abroad. In 1867, Baker's Chocolate and Cocoa won an award in the Paris Exhibition for the quality of the product. In 1873, the company won the highest awards at the Vienna Exhibition, and in 1876, at the Philadelphia Centennial, Walter Baker Chocolate and Cocoa won the highest awards. With mill managers and mill employees, Pierce was able to expand the chocolate business and build new mills. In 1894, these were equipped with chocolate-making machines, most of which were imported from Germany, saved power and were easy to attend.

Pierce followed in his father's footsteps and was elected to the Massachusetts House of Representatives, serving from 1860 to 1862 and again in 1866. He also served in the Forty-third and Forty-fourth Congresses, from 1873 to 1877. His interest in not only his employees but also the voters of Dorchester made him a very popular choice. After Dorchester was annexed to the city of Boston on January 4, 1870, Pierce was nominated and elected mayor of Boston in 1872 and 1877. It was during his terms as mayor that Pierce's business began an extensive marketing and public relations campaign to make Walter Baker & Company a household name or, better, the household choice for chocolate and cocoa. In 1883, the company formally adopted the trademark La Belle Chocolatière as its logo. Used earlier in the company's history, this famous design was copied from the pastel portrait of *Das Schokoladenmadchen* by Jean-Etienne Liotard, an eighteenth-century Swiss painter. The chocolate girl was to become as famous as the company she promoted. In 1884, the trustees of the Baker estate allowed Pierce to purchase the company outright. Once done, it was incorporated as Walter Baker & Company, Ltd.

Pierce was honored by the City of Boston when the school committee voted, in 1892, to name the new grammar school just south of Codman Square in his honor. The school was designed by Boston city architect Harrison H. Atwood (1863–1954) and was an enormous hammered granite building at the corner of Washington Street and Welles Avenue (now the site of the Codman Square Branch of the Boston Public Library). It was considered one of the most advanced schools in the Boston public school system, and after the Great Depression, its focus became that of a "baking school," which offered trade classes.

During Pierce's ownership of the Baker Chocolate Company from 1854 to 1896, he increased business greatly, so much so that he created an urban mill village with modern chocolate mills along the Neponset River. His budget for advertising and marketing was tremendous, but none was more important than the adoption of La Belle Chocolatière as his trademark. He employed women to dress as the trademark come to life in silk gowns, with crisply starched white lawn aprons, caps and cuffs. They would act as demonstrators at exhibitions and fairs, where they offered samples of Baker's Chocolate to those in attendance. These demonstrators, with comely faces and ready smiles, were an important and appropriate way to advertise his product. An article in the *New York Times* on October 21, 1892, reports that these demonstrators were at an exhibition at the Madison Square Garden in New York City, where it was said that the "taste of the chocolate is its own sufficient advertisement, but the combination of chocolate and girl is particularly effective." The article went on to say that at this food show,

> *one of the most noticeable exhibits of this sort is made by Walter Baker & Co., who occupy a conspicuous place just opposite the main entrance to the amphitheatre. Under a silken canopy, disposed as was the canopy at old Ashby, wherein Lady Rowena watched the conquering arms of the young King Ivanhoe, a cluster of pleasing damsels dispenses the soothing "tap"*

of Baker. All are dressed in the costume of "La Belle Chocolatiere" of Liotard's painting in the Dresden Gallery, made familiar to everybody as the trademark of this old established firm. The soft draperies of the canopy are a pleasing frame for the quaint costumes and brilliant complexions of the chocolate girls, and even rival exhibitors praise the taste shown by the firm in displaying its wares so attractively.

These comely demonstrators, who elicited the praise of even the rival exhibitors at an exhibition, were only one aspect of Henry Lillie Pierce's astute ability to attract attention to his products.

Upon his death, Henry Lillie Pierce remembered each and every one of his employees with a gift of $100. His public bequests included one to Harvard that, at the time, was the largest such gift the college had ever received. Pierce also left equal sums to the Museum of Fine Arts, the Massachusetts Institute of Technology, the Massachusetts General Hospital and the Homeopathic Hospital, and it was said that "not in a long time has there been known such generous remembrances of public institutions and charities as in the provisions of his will."

The Baker Mills and other mills along the Neponset River at Dorchester Lower Mills were painted by noted Boston School artist Ernest N. Townsend (1893–1945) in 1911. *Collection of Anthony Sammarco and Cesidio Cedrone.*

WILLIAM MONROE TROTTER

William Monroe Trotter, a resident of Dorchester's Jones Hill neighborhood, was a leading civil rights leader and journalist at the turn of the twentieth century. His life, though short, was dedicated to bringing about the recognition of the achievements of African Americans in this country.

Raised in the town of Hyde Park, William Monroe Trotter (1872–1934) was the son of James Monroe Trotter, a schoolteacher who had served as a lieutenant in the Fifty-fifth Regiment of the Massachusetts Voluntary Infantry during the Civil War. This company was composed of African Americans who enlisted in the Civil War, and Trotter was a well-respected

William Monroe Trotter (1872–1934) was a graduate of Harvard University in 1895 and the first African American member of Phi Beta Kappa. His newspaper, the *Guardian*, was a vitally important voice of the African American community in Boston. In 1969, the City of Boston dedicated a school to his memory on Humboldt Avenue in Roxbury.

member of Company G. His son attended Hyde Park High School, serving as valedictorian of his class. He entered Harvard in 1890 and graduated in 1894, magna cum laude; he was elected to Phi Beta Kappa, a prestigious fraternity of which he was the first African American member. His friendship with William E.B. Du Bois, who was studying for his doctorate at Harvard, extended well into their careers as civil rights leaders. Du Bois, a graduate of Williams College, was the first African American to be awarded a doctorate from Harvard.

Following his graduation from Harvard, Trotter began his career as a real estate broker in Boston. However, in 1901, he founded the *Guardian*, a newspaper somewhat critical of the treatment of people of color. The main purpose of the newspaper, in Trotter's words, was "propaganda against discrimination based on color and denial of citizenship rights because of color." Trotter was a crusader and a born leader in this movement, and he chose for his newspaper office the building that William Lloyd Garrison, an ardent abolitionist, used for the publication of his antislavery newspaper, the *Liberator*, and also where *Uncle Tom's Cabin* was first printed. Trotter's editorship of the *Guardian* was respected, but he led a precarious life that required great self-denial. Trotter said of his chosen career that

> *the conviction grew upon me that pursuit of business, money, civic or literary position was like building a house upon sands; if race prejudice and persecution and public discrimination for mere color was to spread up from the South and result in a fixed caste of color…every colored American would be really a civil outcast, forever an alien, in public life.*

His newspaper and his ardent belief in equality made him a respected citizen of this country. In 1905, with the assistance of Du Bois, he founded the Niagara Movement in New York, the forerunner of what we now know as the National Association for the Advancement of Colored People (NAACP).

Trotter was a dedicated editor of his newspaper. He received great support from his wife, Geraldine L. Pindell, whom he married in 1899; they moved to 97 Sawyer Avenue in Dorchester. Geraldine Trotter's family had been ardent supporters of the desegregation of the Boston Public Schools in the 1850s, and her family encouraged her to attend college. Her support of her husband contributed to an apparently idyllic marriage. Their home, which still stands and has been declared a National Historic Landmark, looked out

Fellow Townsmen of Dorchester

Members of the Niagara Movement, founded by William Monroe Trotter, were superimposed in a photograph in front of a roaring Niagara Falls in New York. Named for the "mighty current of change" the group wanted to effect and for Niagara Falls, which was near where the first meeting took place in July 1905, the Niagara Movement was the precursor of the National Association for the Advancement of Colored People (NAACP).

"over all the country as far as Blue Hill and from my bedroom window over all the bay down to the red buildings on Deer Island," said Trotter. This stable home life enabled him to become the "watchdog" of discrimination, as he became known.

Throughout his life, he was assisted and supported by his wife, who worked with him in the weekly publishing of the *Guardian*. Her interests ran from the support of St. Monica's Home for elderly black women to petitioning the government to make African Americans serving in World War I more comfortable. Geraldine's death in 1918 during the influenza epidemic caused a void in her husband's life, and the editorial page of the *Guardian* had a dedication for the next sixteen years to this woman "who helped...so loyally, faithfully, conscientiously, unselfishly." Following World War I, Trotter led a delegation to Washington to protest the treatment of African Americans who were employed by the government. He was later to attend the Peace Conference in Paris as a delegate of the National Equal Rights League, which tried to outlaw discrimination.

William Monroe Trotter dedicated his life not only to the full participation of African Americans in life but also to their self-realization, to the understanding that they, too, had opinions and should be allowed to express them freely. Trotter's life after his wife's death was precarious, and he was often bothered by the many problems facing him. He once said, "My burdens are more than I can bear, you don't understand, you see one side, the public another side, but I see the third side."

In 1969, the City of Boston named a public grammar school at 35 Humboldt Avenue in Roxbury in memory of William Monroe Trotter, and his home in Dorchester was named a National Historic Landmark. His career, though controversial at times, proved that he really did see the "third side," the side that had made him an ardent journalist, a civil rights leader, the "watchdog" of discrimination and one of Dorchester's proudest sons.

EDWIN J. LEWIS JR.

Edwin J. Lewis Jr. was a noted architect in Boston a century ago. He was said to be a shy and retiring man, but the fact that he designed over thirty-five churches in the United States and Canada makes him one of the more important architects to have called Milton home. As Mary Fifield King, a friend and resident of one of his houses in Milton, said upon his death, "In his profession as an architect he won a high place, and his buildings of great refinement, especially of churches in which he excelled, are found all over New England and beyond."

The son of Edwin and Sarah Richards Lewis, Edwin J. Lewis Jr. (1859–1937) was born in Roxbury. His father emigrated from England and was a successful manufacturer of pickles in Boston. He built a mansion on Adams Street in Dorchester. Educated at the English High School, Lewis attended the Massachusetts Institute of Technology (MIT), which had the first school of architecture in this country, founded in 1867 by William Rotch Ware. Upon his graduation in 1881, he secured a position with the noted Boston architectural firm of Peabody & Stearns. In 1887, he established his own architectural practice, at 9 Park Street on Beacon Hill, and for the next five decades he created a thriving practice "where he continued to go daily during his long professional life." Lewis was to become a post medievalist with his personal interpretation of architecture, be it a residence, meeting hall or place of worship, drawing his inspiration from the medieval period in England. With half-timbered Tudor Revival houses, he recreated, albeit

Edwin J. Lewis Jr. (1859–1937) graduated from MIT and served an apprenticeship with the Boston architectural firm of Peabody & Stearns. From 1887 until his death, he maintained an independent architectural practice at 9 Park Street on Beacon Hill, designing residences of great refinement and over forty Unitarian churches in the United States and Canada.

with Victorian comforts and conveniences, the seventeenth-century aspect of architecture brought to this country by the Puritans when they settled Massachusetts Bay Colony in 1630.

Mrs. King said of him, "His work was a good work and his way straight and honorable." However, unlike many architects, he was financially independent and could chose his clients, many of whom were fellow Unitarians, as he was a leading member of the American Unitarian Association. A member of the First Parish in Dorchester on Meeting House Hill, he designed the vestry built in 1912 to the rear of the Cabot, Everett & Chandler–designed church, which was built in 1897 as a high-style Georgian Revival meetinghouse after a fire destroyed the 1816 church. Over the course of fifty years, Lewis

Beaumont Street, which extends from Carruth to Adams Street, was originally the carriage drive to Beechmont. Herbert Shaw Carruth subdivided his father's estate and had architect-designed houses built, or stipulated to be built, to create an elegant and well-planned neighborhood of Victorian Boston.

was to design impressive, random ashlar quarry-faced stone and wood-shingle churches that echoed back to an earlier architectural period and might be considered modified Gothic Revival designs. In Dorchester, he designed Christ Church Unitarian at Dorchester Avenue and Dix Street, and the Peabody, a massive apartment and professional building at Peabody Square commissioned by the Episcopal Diocese of Massachusetts; he also designed the Dedham Historical Society, the Hopedale Community House, All Souls' Church in Braintree, the Roslindale Unitarian (now St. Anna's Orthodox) Church and the First Church of Christ Scientist in Quincy. He designed and built over forty houses that I have identified in Dorchester, as well as five in Milton.

Lewis was a noted and popular lecturer on history, architectural history and ecclesiastical topics and was an active worker in the city for municipal reform, especially the City Conservation League. He and his two sisters, Bertha and Marion Lewis, lived in the family mansion in Dorchester until 1923, when they moved to 121 Canton Avenue in Milton. Surprisingly, this important architect never lived in a house of his own design. In his fifty years as an independent architect, Lewis maintained memberships in the American Institute of Architects, the Boston Society of Architects (where he served as secretary), the Boston Athenaeum and the Union Club. He also served as president of the Dorchester Historical Society from 1917 to 1921. Erudite, educated and well informed, he "lived on the gentler side of life, with books and art and the higher interests of his city, and Boston owes him much."

As Mrs. King said in her tribute to her late friend, "Mr. Lewis would not have asked for tears nor for praise, but for appreciation, perhaps, with esteem and lasting friendships, and these he had."

Edward A. Huebener

Edward A. Huebener (1851–1936) was born prior to the annexation of Dorchester to the city of Boston, and he was understandably affected by the issues involved. Undoubtedly, he saw many of the old Dorchester estates being demolished for subdivisions at the turn of the twentieth century. The story of his mother asking for a brick to stop the door from slamming is a charming answer to his obvious fetish for brick collecting, but the collection is remarkable in its scope and its diversity.

Edward Huebener was apprenticed as an upholsterer and woodcarver to an F. Schlotterback, and by 1890 he had a "hospital" for antiques in his shop on Adams Street, in King Square, Dorchester. He was born in the Old Danforth House near Meeting House Hill on Bowdoin Street, securing a brick from this house at the time of its demolition. His life was one of constant pursuit of local history, and the letters "EAH" are a trademark that marks many of the photographs and antiques in the collections of Historic New England and the Dorchester Historical Society. Huebener was the son of John George and Mary Alhit Huebener, who were born in Holland and France, respectively. His love of local history has great meaning; he was born in the former Turks Head Tavern near Meeting House Hill, and his interest may have been nurtured by the charms afforded by the history of an old house. The Reverend John Danforth built the tavern in 1680, and the noted author of *The Lamplighter*, Miss Maria Cummins, lived here with her father, Judge Cummins, in the nineteenth century. Later, the Huebeners moved to

Freeport Street at Glover's Corner. It was in this house that the now famous request of Mrs. Huebener was heard: "Bring some bricks to keep the doors from slamming!" This story has now become history.

As a young man, Huebener courted and then married Amanda A. Christmas of Brighton. Their wedding took place on September 4, 1884, at All Saints Episcopal Church, Ashmont. They had one child, Elizabeth A. Huebener, who shared her father's obvious love of local history. In 1890, Huebener established his own shop at 315 Adams Street, Dorchester. He was well known for his steam-cleaning techniques on carpets and for the reproduction of tabernacle mirrors. He was a lover of old things—his interest was sincere—and his collection of hand-painted bricks increased in both size and scope through the words: "Madam, may I have a brick from the chimney of this house?" Later, Huebener had a "furniture hospital" at 76 Parkman Street in King Square, and he lived nearby at 80 Parkman Street. Huebener's eccentric personality intensified as he aged. According to one well-respected lady of this venerable town, he not only made his own coffin of well-seasoned hardwood but also occasionally slept in it. It seemed interesting, though unusual, to sleep in a coffin, especially since his family opted, after his death due to pneumonia and senility, to cremate his remains at the Forest Hills Crematorium.

Huebener will forever remain a well-respected local antiquarian. He was a vice-president of the Bay State Historical League, a director of the Dorchester Historical Society and a contributing member of the Society for the Preservation of New England Antiquities (now known as Historic New England). His death marked the passing of an era, as many of our details and facts of Dorchester went with him. We revere his contributions to the preservation and dissemination of Dorchester history. Huebener was an authority on the history and the architectural design of each individual house depicted in the bricks. Many times, it is related, he would produce a spiel of interesting facts that made these lumps of baked clay come to life.

H. EUGENE BOLLES

No trip to New York City is complete for me without a trip to visit the Metropolitan Museum of Art on the Upper East Side. Its collection of paintings, sculpture and decorative arts are superb, but what interests me most is the collection of American Decorative Arts, which have a strong connection to Dorchester.

In 1909, the Met hosted an exhibit of American Decorative Arts, known as the Hudson-Fulton Exhibit, in recognition of the 300th anniversary of the founding of New York. The exhibit included furniture, paintings, pottery, glass and textiles in one of the most important retrospective exhibits ever held in the United States up to that time. Among the numerous lenders to the exhibit, which attracted a record 300,000 people, was H. Eugene Bolles, a resident of Dorchester.

Hezekiah Eugene Bolles (1853–1910), a graduate of Boston University Law School and a noted attorney in Boston, lived in a grand house at 401 Quincy Street in Dorchester. The son of William and Cornelia Congdon Palmer Bolles, he was born on Bolles Hill in New London, Connecticut, and moved to Dorchester in 1882, when he married Elizabeth Clapp

Hezekiah Eugene Bolles, Esq. (1853–1910), was a successful attorney and antique collector. He sold his unparalleled collection of American and English antiques to the Metropolitan Museum of Art in New York, where it became an important addition to the Decorative Arts collection. *Courtesy Winterthur Library.*

Howe (1853–1920), daughter of James and Martha Neal Jenkins Howe of Dorchester. After their marriage, in 1885, Elizabeth and H. Eugene Bolles commissioned local architect John A. Fox (1835–1920) to design a large house at the crest of Quincy and Bellevue Streets, just up the hill from Columbia Street (now Columbia Road). They lived like other affluent Dorchester families in the post-annexation years, except that they added to their family heirlooms, inherited by Mrs. Bolles from her Dorchester ancestors, with fine examples of furniture, glass, china and textiles from the early seventeenth century to the Federal period. Bolles, who had begun collecting fine antiques in the early 1880s, was so serious a collector that he was a founder of the Walpole Society, along with Henry Knight and Luke Vincent Lockwood, a scholarly group of museum curators, professionals and above-average collectors who met at fellow members' homes, museums and historic houses for private and in-depth tours and lectures.

The Bolles House was literally crammed with furniture ranging in style from Pilgrim chests and chairs, Court cupboards and Chippendale highboys, lowboys and chairs to high-style Federal card tables, chairs and sofas. Not only was the house furnished with museum-quality antiques, but they were also stored in the attic and in an off-site storeroom. Interestingly, the Bolleses not only had a deep appreciation and increasing awareness of their collection, but also they actually used it on a daily basis, which is a remarkably healthy attitude for someone who collects antiques. During the year leading up to the New York exhibit, the Bolleses were often visited by Henry W. Kent, a friend who was also an assistant to Robert de Forest, secretary to the museum and chairman of the celebration committee on art exhibits. Kent was on friendly terms with many early art and antique collectors who had amassed important collections, such as George S. Palmer, R.T.H. Halsey, Alphonse Clearwater and H. Eugene Bolles, who was induced by his friend to loan forty-one objects to the exhibit.

H. Eugene Bolles and his wife came to the realization that their collection of American Decorative Arts, which spanned the period from 1630 to 1815, was not only an important collection with a wide spectrum of styles and objects but also that it should be preserved intact. Following the exhibit, Bolles was induced by Henry Kent to sell the collection, which encompassed 434 pieces of furniture and included "miscellaneous objects ranging from cooking utensils to fire buckets and helmets," to the Met, where it was displayed in period room settings and like-object exhibitions. Unfortunately, even though the Bolleses' collection was preserved intact, they sold it to the museum rather than donating it; the collection was actually purchased by the museum with funds donated by Mrs. Russell Sage (1828–1918), a wealthy benefactor of the museum. Thus, the collection is known today as the Sage Collection rather than the Bolles Collection. To Kent, who must have been ecstatic in having secured the Bolles Collection for the museum, H. Eugene Bolles wrote in a letter, "We hope…that before long we shall have the pleasure of another visit from you. If we have no chairs for you to sit in, you will understand the reason why, and I am sure under the circumstances will not object to sitting on the front stairs." With such a vast amount of antique furniture shipped from Dorchester to New York, one can imagine how empty the house on Quincy Street actually was.

So, the next time you are in New York, plan to stop by the Met and visit its impressive Decorative Arts Collection. While admiring these premier pieces of American craftsmanship, remember that it was the discerning eye, diligent collecting skills and tenacity of a fellow Dorchesterite that ensured his collection would be enjoyed by the public after his death. Maybe I'll see you there!

6

BUSINESS AND INDUSTRY

CREHORE & FORD PLAYING CARD FACTORY

The nation's oldest public school and Boston's oldest house are both located in Dorchester. The Neponset River, which divides Dorchester from Quincy and Milton, is also home to two historical firsts: the first paper manufactured in the American colonies was made just across the river in Milton, and the first playing cards in the United States were made on River Street in Dorchester Lower Mills.

Paper was manufactured as early as 1728 on the Neponset River in Milton by Boies and McLean, two enterprising businessmen who turned discarded rags into pulp that was processed into rag paper, or parchment, which was used for not only writing paper but also legal documents, wills and even printed currency. As the first manufacturers of paper in this country, not only was the paper mill a busy one, but it was also an immensely profitable one. At the turn of the nineteenth century, Amor Hollingsworth and Edmund Pitt Tileston bought the mill. Producing the same fine rag paper as the mill's founders, the Tileston & Hollingsworth Paper Mill added the manufacture of newsprint and wrapping and card stock paper. Each of these new forms of paper was used by various manufacturers, but the card stock was used by Crehore & Ford, a playing card manufactory in Dorchester. Playing cards had been known in this country since the eighteenth century, but invariably they were of either English or French manufacture and were often said to be "profane with the instruments of perdition." The cards were imprinted with the four suits—the ace, heart, spade and clover—but not with numbers.

The Thomas Crehore House was on River Street at the present site of Shaw's Supermarket. In an ell in the rear of the house, Thomas Crehore and Jaziniah Ford produced the first playing cards in the United States.

Games such as chance, or loo, were played with small pieces of mother of pearl used as chips if it was a betting game.

By the 1790s, the playing of cards, earlier condemned by Puritans as immoral, had become a popular recreation, and it was only a matter of time before they were produced in this country. Partners Thomas Crehore and Jaziniah Ford went into business as Crehore & Ford on River Street, the present site of Shaw's Supermarket. Thomas Crehore (1769–1846) had a three-story Federal house with a large ell, or wing, in the rear where colorful playing cards were printed. So proud of their playing cards were Crehore and Ford that most were imprinted with "American Manufacture" and had such images as the battle between the *Constitution* and the *Guerrière* during the War of 1812; President George Washington; and the Marquis de Lafayette, who visited the United States in 1824, traveled throughout the country and was fêted in every city and town he stopped in.

This playing card by Crehore & Ford depicts the Queen of Diamonds. This early nineteenth-century playing card was colorful but crudely printed, and it was without numbers, only using suits for card games of loo or chance.

Jaziniah Ford (1757–1832) eventually left Crehore and produced playing cards in a small card factory on Highland Street in Milton. Thomas Crehore continued to produce these now valuable playing cards in the ell on River Street in Dorchester Lower Mills until the manufactory was destroyed by fire. So the next time you decide to play solitaire—or heaven forbid, old maid—think of the history you hold in your hands, and good luck!

THE TUTTLE HOUSE

The Puritans who settled Dorchester in 1630 first landed at Savin Hill. Rowing in longboats from Hull, a party of the settlers came upon the marshes at Fox Point, while the remaining settlers walked along the coastline from Hull to Mattapanock, the Indian name for Dorchester. The site was known

Savin Hill, shown here in an etching of the original 1830 landscape painting by Michael Olcott Barry (1813–1858), was once known as Rock Hill and later Old Hill, before being renamed in 1822 by Joseph Tuttle for the *Juniperus sabina*, the columnar savin juniper tree that once proliferated the hill. Barry was said to be a "gentleman by nature and education [who] with a rare suavity of manners blended ease with elegance."

as Rock Hill in the seventeenth century, due to the numerous outcroppings of stone, and later as Old Hill, because this was among the earliest sites of the settlement. At the crest of the hill was once located the fort, which served to protect the settlers in case of attack by sea.

The Savin Hill area had always been pleasant, with proximity to Dorchester Bay and views of the harbor. With its tall trees and lush vegetation, in 1855 it was viewed as being "the same grouping of cedars and the same magnificent rocks...the same fine view of the harbor" that Edward Everett had seen as a child in Dorchester. However, the area did change, for in 1822 Joseph Tuttle (1786–1870) purchased the old Wiswall House on Savin Hill Avenue (originally Green Lane) and remodeled the property as an early "seaside hotel." Joseph Tuttle was a successful mason who lived in Boston. He purchased the property in Dorchester as a business venture and immediately added two wings to the house. He began to advertise in Boston newspapers for people to visit the "Tuttle House," which was on the stagecoach line from Boston to Neponset, a pleasant ride of three miles and twelve and a half cents each way. The Tuttle House became famous for its chicken dinners and for its special attention to sleighing parties in the winter.

A seaside hotel within three miles of Boston made for a popular site and was sure to attract summer residents. Tuttle added stables, cottages, bowling saloons and an icehouse to ensure his guests' every comfort. The hotel, located at what are now Savin Hill Avenue and Tuttle Street, was adjacent to the Old Colony Railroad when it was put through Dorchester, connecting Boston with the South Shore towns. Tuttle, who obviously had a flair for marketing, decided to rename the area Savin Hill after the numerous columnar cedars that covered the hill. These trees, a species of conifers, no longer grow on Savin Hill, but they once made an impressive backdrop to the popular seaside hotel and the luxurious villas that were being built along Savin Hill Avenue.

The Tuttle House not only served dinners but also accommodated overnight and weekly guests, and Joseph Tuttle was "widely known as a genial host." The rooms were not overly abundant, with but a half dozen to serve the needs of the hotel. The entrance was met by the original stairway that led to the third-floor ballroom, where both hotel guests and local residents

The Tuttle House was at the corner of Savin Hill Avenue and Tuttle Street and was one of the first seaside hotels in the Boston area. Joseph Tuttle's hotel became known for its delicious chicken dinners and for its special attention to sleighing parties in the winter months.

could dance while musicians played from the wide platform. The hotel, originally conceived of as a seaside hotel, later accommodated residents who lived at the Tuttle House for many years. By the later part of the nineteenth century, Savin Hill, as all of Dorchester, saw tremendous growth through the development of the farms and estates for residential blocks. The Tuttle House, maintaining a few acres of open land, began to be surrounded by houses built on the new streets named Sagamore, Saxton, Tuttle and Sydney. The City of Boston erected a bandstand on the front lawn for lawn concerts, which were enjoyed by both the resident guests and their neighbors. The old hotel was bounded by new streets, but the open lawns enclosed by wood fences allowed sunlight to shine on the now historic and venerable hotel.

The Tuttle House, once patronized by the wealthiest and most fashionable Bostonians, had become a large residential hotel on prime land. The area of Savin Hill had seen great changes, and the Tuttle family deemed that it should be sold. In 1924, the resident manager, Mr. Cole, vacated the Tuttle House, and the house was razed. The once fashionable seaside hotel was gone, and the site was to become St. William's School. The Archdiocese of Boston had purchased the land and, having built a large school on the site, continued to make the land available for the public's use—in this case, for education.

The Tuttle House, though gone for decades, could have been the subject of the following loving but anonymous observation: "It is not the sunshine or any other tangible way that accounts for the pleasantness of old house corners. In the cheeriness and the pleasantness that clustered there, the very walls drunk them in."

TALBOT'S GROCERY STORE

Talbot's Grocery Store in Dorchester Lower Mills had provided over a century of service in staple and fancy goods to the residents of Dorchester and Milton when it closed in 1919. John Talbot opened his store in 1815 on the Dorchester side of the Neponset River next to the bridge to Milton. The Dorchester Turnpike (now Avenue) was cut through the town in 1804, terminating at the Lower Mills. So the store was on the major crossroads between Boston and the towns on the South Shore and had a large amount of trade from travelers. Also, the store's proximity to both residential areas and the mills made its success almost immediate.

Talbot's Grocery Store was on Washington Street in the Dorchester Lower Mills, between Adams and River Streets. First opened in 1815 at the bridge crossing the Neponset River, it was moved in 1848 to Washington Street, where it not only provided grocery staples but was also said to be the leading supplier of rum and intoxicants in the Lower Mills.

Supplying most of the necessities to shoppers in the village, Talbot's was also the leading supplier of rum and intoxicants. Almost 90 percent of the business concerned liquor, which, reputedly, was sold "only to those not in impoverished circumstances." In fact, the store stocked expensive wines and liquors, most of which were out of the reach of the poor. Outgrowing the original store, in 1848 Talbot's moved the one-story building to Washington Street, near River Street on the present site of Metamorphosis of Lower Mills. The store was remodeled, and a second story and large front porch were added on. One feature of Talbot's Store was a reading room in which residents could peruse newspapers, journals and books or simply debate questions of local importance. It seemed that Talbot's not only attracted a steady clientele but was also a place for friends to stop by.

Lower Mills was a busy area in the years prior to the Civil War, with numerous mills along the Neponset River providing employment for local residents. A stagecoach, operated by the Dunmore Brothers, ran to Boston daily at a cost of twelve and a half cents each way. The mills, operated by Baker Chocolate, Preston Chocolate and the Webb & Twombley Chocolate

Companies, produced such a quantity of the delicious staple that the area was often referred to as Chocolate Village.

The residential area mushroomed as a direct result of the mill development and the accessibility of Lower Mills via the Old Colony Railroad, which started running in 1848 with the Dorchester and Milton Branch serving the area along the river through a depot at Mattapan Square. As a result, Talbot's Store attracted customers as not only a convenient store but one that provided the fancy goods usually available only in Boston. The friendly atmosphere in Talbot's Store is recounted by the late Virginia Holbrook:

> *For a number of years we used cane-seated chairs of cherry wood in the dining room. A blind man wove new seats when necessary. The customer was responsible for delivering and calling for the work. One day when I was walking home with Grandpa* [retired developer Silas Pinckney Holbrook of Holbrook & Fox] *and he was carrying a newly caned chair, we stopped at Talbot's Grocery store. Grandpa set the chair down and sat upon it, remarking to the store's two clerks, "I always carry a chair with me when I go walking so that I may sit and rest when I get tired." The head salesman, Fred Preston, saw the joke, but the humor escaped the serious-minded helper Charlie Chaddock.*

The family-owned Talbot's Store was served by three generations. In 1890, the grandson and namesake of the founder entered the business. Retaining the aspects that made the store famous, John Talbot III continued to stock Talbot's with high-quality groceries and liquors. During World War I, the store was able to stock the necessities for its customers when most stores were unable to obtain even small amounts of flour, sugar and salt. But competition from new grocery stores was heating up in the early twentieth century, and Talbot, who was nearing retirement age, decided to close the business. When Talbot's Grocery Store closed in 1919, another well-known landmark ceased to exist.

ROSWELL GLEASON BRITANNIA WORKS

When we think of silver plate, the names Reed & Barton, Rogers and Lunt come to mind. Few of us realize that the first attempts at silver plating base metal in this country took place on Washington Street, near Four Corners, in the mid-nineteenth century.

Roswell Gleason (1799–1881) was a successful manufacturer of Britannia ware and was among the first in this country to silver plate base metal, which looked as if it was made from the finest solid silver. Gleason's adaptation to changing public tastes enabled him to revel in phenomenal success. His portrait shows, through the draped window, his factory and showroom in Dorchester. *Courtesy of Shelburne Museum, gift in 2010 by Anthony M. Sammarco and Cesidio L. Cedrone.*

Roswell Gleason (1799–1887) was born in Putney, Vermont, the son of Reuben and Abigail Fuller Gleason, but came to Dorchester as a young apprentice to William Wilcox, a tinsmith at Four Corners. In 1822, after Wilcox's death, Gleason was able to conduct business on his own. His shop produced tin and pewter items that were used in every home of the period, but it was the introduction of Britannia that brought fame to Gleason. Britannia is a pewter alloy composed of lead, tin and other metals to form a pliable metal that withstands constant use. Gleason, through melding and experimentation, made a large array of Britannia ware serving pieces that had a more durable quality than the softer pewter. His business was successful enough that he moved from the former Wilcox shop to a new factory at the present site of Mother's Rest.

The new factory employed numerous workmen and was to produce a high-quality Britannia ware that was not only sold locally but was also shipped by barge, boat and train throughout the eastern seaboard. Gleason produced lamps that held whale oil, teapots and coffeepots and caster sets that became a staple in most households; the design and quality of his products brought the attention of buyers from Stowell & Company and Lows, Ball & Company, two fashionable Boston shops.

However, it was in the late 1840s that Gleason learned of beautiful wares that had a polished surface that made them look as if they were made from the finest solid silver. Urged by his friend Daniel Webster, Gleason sent his sons, Roswell Gleason Jr. (1826–1866) and Edward Gleason (1829–1862), to England to study the process of silver plating. They returned after a short while with not only the knowledge to produce silver-plated metal but also with English workmen who were trained and skillful in the process. "In 1849 he…increased his business by introducing the art of silver plating, and was the pioneer of that business in America." With the establishment of this new line in his already successful business, Roswell Gleason made

R. GLEASON & SONS,

Manufacturers of and Wholesale Dealers in

SILVER PLATED WARE,

COMPRISING

TEA SETS, URNS, CASTORS,

CAKE BASKETS, PITCHERS, &C.

WASHINGTON STREET, DORCHESTER, MASS.

ROSWELL GLEASON.   ROSWELL GLEASON, JR.   EDWARD GLEASON.

This 1868 advertisement from the *Dorchester and Quincy Directory* for R. Gleason & Sons, "Manufacturers of and Wholesale Dealers in Silver Plated Ware," shows the factory (left) and the showroom on Washington Street near Four Corners. Gleason and his sons oversaw well-trained employees who made silver-plated cruets, pitchers, tea and coffee services and serving pieces at a fraction of the cost of solid silver, yet they shone just as brightly on a hostess's table.

silver tea services available for those with fancy tastes but not the money to purchase solid silver services. With the availability of silver plate, Gleason revolutionized the silver industry and made cruets, pitchers, services and serving pieces available at a fraction of the cost of solid silver.

It was precisely the ability of Gleason's adaptation to changing public tastes and the changing methods of production that enabled him to revel in phenomenal success. His career was successful, and he was fortunate in his family, for he married Rebecca Tucker Vose (1805–1891) of Milton, daughter of Reuben and Polly Willis Vose, and built a splendid mansion, known as Lilacs, for her in 1837. His success as a businessman allowed him the finest material comforts, and his large Gothic villa was on Washington Street, just south of his factory. The house was one of the finest in Dorchester, with superb panoramic views of Dorchester Bay from the piazzas. It was complete with a stable and grapery and had white lilacs planted about the property from cuttings secured from Mount Vernon, President George Washington's estate in Virginia. With a playing fountain and a large carriage drive, the estate was not just an elegant countryseat but also testimony to Gleason's ability as a businessman. He was listed in the book *Rich Men of Massachusetts* in 1851 and was honored and esteemed in Dorchester. His financial support of the Christopher Gibson School located on School Street was widely appreciated, and he served as captain of the Dorchester Rifle Company, a local drill company composed of Dorchesterites who met at Mount Bowdoin to exchange sham battles and to feast on lavish dinners prepared for the occasion. Gleason was successful and popular, but the deaths of his sons effectively ended his business.

Both of Rebecca and Roswell Gleason's sons died relatively young. The Civil War had ended the shipments of Gleason's wares to southern markets, and an explosion in his factory caused tremendous damage. Unable to continue, Gleason closed the silver plate and Britannia ware factory in 1871 and retired to a life of ease as near a millionaire as had ever been known in Dorchester. He continued his support of local charities, including the Second Church in Codman Square, where he attended both morning and afternoon services every Sunday. He eventually went blind but maintained a sense of duty to the end. His death came suddenly, and he was buried in his family lot in the Codman Cemetery, the parish burial ground of the Second Church on Norfolk Street.

The family—the only surviving child was Mary Frances Gleason Vandervoort (1825–1885)—maintained Lilacs as a virtual museum, with many Gleason-produced items among the family antiques. A fire destroyed a portion of the house, and rather than rebuild, the house was moved to face Dorchester Bay, and the former carriage drive to the stable was cut through and renamed Ridge Road (now Claybourne Street). The wealth amassed by Roswell Gleason during the nineteenth century enabled him to live in comfort and to amass a large estate; however, it was that estate that made the greatest fortune for the family, as after the annexation of Dorchester to the city of Boston in 1870, land values skyrocketed and were the best investment one could make. Lilacs stood atop the hill at the corner of Park and Claybourne Streets, not just as a reminder of the man who built it but also as a monument to the silver-plated empire he created on Washington Street in Dorchester.

J.H. Upham & Company

After the annexation of Dorchester to the city of Boston in 1870, the area known as Upham's Corner became much less of a country crossroads and more of an urban commercial district. The houses and small wood-framed buildings gave way to large commercial buildings and transformed the area into a thriving shopping district.

Upham's Corner was named for Amos Upham, who kept a general store at the corner of Dudley and Boston (now Columbia Road) Streets. The store, with living space above, served the needs of area residents, but "as far back as 1830, Upham's Corner was very sparsely settled and where then were half a dozen houses, there are now hundreds. Cattle grazed in the pastures of farms nearby, where there are houses and streets." Upham moved from Sudbury and married Abigail Humphreys in 1819. They were the parents of numerous children, among them James Humphreys Upham.

J.H. Upham (1820–1890) began in the family business in 1834, serving in many capacities until 1842, when he was made a partner in his father's grocery store. As A. & J.H. Upham Company, they provided teas, coffees and cocoa to the neighborhood, as well as pots, pans and buckets. A general store had to keep a ready supply of all necessities, even though Dorchester's population numbered fewer than six thousand residents in 1842. Continuing in business, the store became a fixture of the crossroads, and as in many Dorchester squares where a merchant kept a general store, the area was

James Humphreys Upham (1820–1890) was the son of Amos Upham, who in the early nineteenth century opened a general store at Upham's Corner. A successful businessman and real estate developer, he also served as the last chairman of the board of selectmen in Dorchester in 1869 and later as a member of the Boston Common Council.

renamed Upham's Corner. (Field's Corner, Glover's Corner and Baker's Corner [now Codman Square] were also named for the merchants in their respective areas.)

James Humphreys Upham was a concerned citizen as well as a successful merchant. According to an 1891 article, he was "chairman of the Board of Selectmen, of the Overseers of the Poor, and the Surveyor of Highways, a member of the School Committee and Assessor for four years. He was twice elected to represent his town in the General Court, and when Dorchester was annexed to the city of Boston he was twice elected to the Common Council." His interests in the town, and his obvious wealth, led him to replace the old store with a one-story brick structure that would later be enlarged to four stories. The first use of electricity in Dorchester was recorded in the Upham Building. This impressive commercial block created an urban aspect to Upham's Corner. Adjacent to the market was Winthrop Hall, a theater and assembly hall that would later be remodeled with an Art Deco façade for the

Mr. and Mrs. J.H. Upham stand in front of the new one-story red brick and granite store built in 1884 at the corner of Boston (later Columbia Road) and Dudley Streets. This store reputedly had the first electric lights in Dorchester. The building later had three more stories added and became known as the Upham Building, or the Columbia Square Building.

Dorchester Savings Bank. Across the street was the five-story Northwood, a residential apartment building that is now the site of the bank and parking lot. As the area became less residential, commercial and multifamily apartment buildings—most of them of impressive design—were built along Dudley Street and the new Columbia Road, which was laid out in the 1890s linking the Strandway in South Boston to Franklin Park.

Upham was instrumental in convincing his fellow residents that annexing the town to Boston would be a positive thing. As chairman of the board of selectmen in Dorchester, he offered numerous reasons to allow the annexation and, once accomplished, set about to develop much of his land into income-generating property. By the time of his death in 1891, James Humphreys Upham was one of the wealthiest residents of Dorchester and could boast of having increased his father's business tenfold. In his obituary, it was said that there "is probably no larger business in the Dorchester district than theirs." The firm of J.H. Upham & Company "has increased until now; the firm has a trade extending over a radius of two miles, having four routes." Though

Upham's Corner was named for Amos Upham (1788–1879) and is the junction of Columbia Road and Stoughton and Dudley Streets, which by the early twentieth century had become an urban crossroads. On the left are the Dorchester, an apartment building; Winthrop Hall; the Upham (often referred to as the Columbia Square Building) Building; and a corner of the S.B. Pierce Building.

the Upham family no longer operates the business in the square named for their ancestor, Upham's Corner is still a thriving commercial district that attracts Dorchesterites on daily business.

THE EDDY REFRIGERATOR COMPANY

Few of us in Dorchester are without a refrigerator in the kitchen, and as last summer's heat waves rolled in, we were especially thankful for its intended purpose. However, few of us know that in 1847, Darius Eddy of Dorchester established the "Eddy refrigerator" in King Square, Dorchester.

Darius Eddy (1809–1893) recognized that people needed refrigeration to cool food and to preserve it for use after it had been brought from the market. An enterprising businessman, he established his company on Gibson Street near Field's Corner to produce ice chests, or wooden boxes with metal linings that held ice to keep food cool. Crafting his "refrigerators" from fine-

EDDY'S STANDARD

REFRIGERATORS

and WOODEN WARE.

Established

1847.

MANUFACTURED AND FOR SALE BY

D. EDDY & SON,

BOSTON, (Dorchester District) MASS., U. S. A.

Near Harrison Sq. Station, on Old Colony Railroad.

1881.

Since 1847, Darius Eddy & Sons manufactured wooden refrigerators that, along with blocks of ice supplied by the local iceman, kept food fresh. Eddy's refrigerators were marketed as "dry, sweet and clean" and were touted as "absolutely the best" refrigerators on the market.

quality wood and lining the sides with steel, Eddy sold these popular cooling units throughout New England. The demand proved great, and though the original factory was destroyed by fire in 1872, Eddy built a new, expanded and more modern facility at King Square, on the corner of Adams and Gibson Streets.

Eddy refrigerators were marketed to be "dry, sweet and clean" and were designed "to protect the health of the family" by the circulation of cold, fresh air through the refrigerator. With almost daily replacement of the ice block by the local iceman, food was kept fresh for longer periods of time. The increase in productivity led to the building of warehouses for stock items and for the display of refrigerators to be sold to the public. Eventually, Eddy's sons assisted him in the business. After 1872, Eddy took his sons Lewis, Isaac and George Eddy into the rapidly growing company. They maintained the use of wood for the cabinets, but after electricity was invented, newer refrigerators were electrified. The Eddy family maintained the old methods of production, which required the daily replacement of ice.

Eventually, Darius Eddy & Sons, marketing their refrigerators as "absolutely the best" on the market, could no longer compete with the larger and more efficient factories that produced electric refrigerators. The firm ceased to exist after World War I, and the factory was sold to Andrews & Goodrich. However, many Eddy-produced ice chests still exist and attest to the fine-quality workmanship of a refrigerator company established over a century and a half ago in Dorchester.

DORCHESTER POTTERY WORKS

The Dorchester Pottery Works was established in 1895 on Preston Street (now Victory Road) and produced hand-decorated stoneware of distinctive New England motifs until its demise in 1979. Founded by George Henderson (1863–1928) on land adjoining the prestigious Harrison Square neighborhood of Dorchester, the pottery works initially produced stoneware for commercial use. Henderson, a native of North Cambridge, had been a partner since 1884 in the firm of S.L. Pewtress Pottery in New Haven, Connecticut, under the style of Henderson and O'Halloran. The decision to sell his partnership and move from New Haven to Dorchester may have been of a family nature, but when he relocated in 1895, he established a family business that would strive for old-fashioned, well-made stoneware.

From 1895 to World War I, the Dorchester Pottery Works produced such items as mash feeders, chicken fountains and cheese crocks, as well as acid pots and dipping baskets for plating and jewelry companies. Also, the patented Henderson Foot warmer, the clay pig and the forerunner of the rubber hot water bottle went on to compose 29 percent of the pottery works' total annual sales by 1919. Adjacent to the Dorchester Pottery Works was Harrison Square, a neighborhood designed and laid out by local architect Luther Briggs Jr. and named after President William Henry Harrison (1773–1841). The area, now referred to as Clam Point, is near Dorchester Bay and the former Old Colony Railroad, which passed through the square. This transportation route enabled Henderson to receive his clay from South

DORCHESTER
POTTERY WORKS

FOUNDED 1890

NEW ENGLAND'S ONLY STONEWARE MANUFACTURERS

01 Victory Road ~ Dorchester, Mass.
~ Tel. TALbot 0810 ~

A catalogue of the Dorchester Pottery Works from 1929 proudly proclaimed that the pottery works was founded in 1890 and, after forty years, was "New England's only stoneware manufacturer." The Henderson family had, for over eight decades, produced both commercial ware and decorative stoneware that were made by the "old-time methods of production."

Amboy, New Jersey, and his cobalt from Germany and to ship his finished products, thus allowing his business to increase and thrive. As the business grew, Henderson obtained a permit in 1910 to construct a new beehive kiln. Designed by him personally, the downdraft kiln was built four years later by specialists from Germany. Measuring twenty-two feet in diameter and ten and a half feet in height, the new kiln allowed for up to three freight carloads of pottery to be fired at one time.

The concept of stoneware is an important one, as it requires three thousand degrees of heat for firing, whereas earthenware only requires fifteen hundred degrees. The stoneware Henderson produced required two weeks of attention. The kiln was fired with a combination of wood and coal for forty-eight hours or until the necessary temperature was attained. Once

Nando Ricci (1911–1998) was a second-generation master potter at the Dorchester Pottery Works. He is seen here stacking bricks that would seal the door to the kiln, after which the pottery would be fired at three-thousand-degree heat. The pottery works was said to have "maintained the high standard of workmanship that characterized the potteries of an earlier day."

reached, the shutters to the fire holes were closed, and the kiln was allowed to cool slowly for five days before the unloading process could begin. The door to the kiln, composed of bricks and mortar, then had to be carefully dismantled. However, before the kiln could even be loaded, the potters had to produce pieces from clay. With wheels and molds, bean pots, casseroles, dishes, jugs and mixing bowls took shape, along with the industrial goods being produced. By 1925, there were twenty-eight employees with six potters and three salesmen.

Charles Wilson Henderson, the founder's son, and his wife, Ethel Hill Henderson, assisted the family business from World War I until the death of George Henderson in 1928. The couple reevaluated the Dorchester Pottery Works at this crucial time, adding new lines of decorative tableware to augment those already in production. The Great Depression caused the business to suffer, as the pottery works' most important customers were the factories affected by the harsh business decline. To compete with other pottery companies, Ethel Hill Henderson began to decorate her stoneware with motifs of old New England. Before her marriage in 1919, Ethel had been an industrial arts teacher at Dorchester High School and had designed fabrics and colonial revival motifs in her spare time. By adding to the stoneware decorations of pinecones, blueberries, strawberries, lily of the valley, pussy willow, the sacred cod and spouting sperm whales, Ethel Henderson revolutionized the Dorchester Pottery Works, breathing new life into the business. The stoneware—fashioned on a wheel, hand dipped in sealer and then hand decorated—was produced through a time-consuming and labor-intensive process. However, the result was stoneware that literally said "Dorchester Pottery."

Whereas the commercial ware lines so important in the early years of the works were undecorated and purely functional pieces, the decorative pieces could hold their own when compared to well-known Dedham Pottery, another Boston-area pottery business. Charles Allen Hill, Ethel's brother, also came to work for the business. Hill had been a chemistry teacher prior to joining the Dorchester Pottery Works, and his color mixing was of superior quality. This family affair was further augmented by Ethel's sister, Lillian Hill Yeaton, who assisted in the sales end of the business. Charles and Ethel Henderson began a series of stoneware lines that made the pottery a veritable museum of design. After World War II, Ethel traveled to Mount Vernon, where she re-created an eighteenth-century hanging herb pot like one used by President George Washington. Glazed but undecorated, it was supplied to the gift shop at Mount Vernon for many years, as were stoneware mugs for Radcliffe College and the Tufts Dental School. Roommates at the colleges were given identical mugs, with handles of different scraffito designs, which allowed their use without confusion. The decorative stoneware grew to make up the majority of production revenues, while the manufacture of commercial ware dwindled.

In the 1960s, the labor-intensive business was recognized as one that still employed "old-time methods of production." Lura Woodside Watkins, a noted authority on American decorative arts, wrote that the Dorchester Pottery Works "alone maintained the high standard of workmanship that characterized the potteries of an earlier day." With the last firing of the huge custom-built kiln in 1965, the final decline of the Dorchester Pottery Works began. The beehive kiln was replaced by a smaller gas-fired one that proved more efficient and economical but took away some of the charm of workmanship. The death of Charles W. Henderson in 1967 struck the death knell of the business, as for the next twelve years his survivors simply produced enough pottery to keep the works going. Carried on by his widow and her brother and sister, and ably assisted by the last potter, Nando Ricci, the Dorchester Pottery Works was one of the few stoneware factories founded in the nineteenth century that still remained.

After Ethel Hill Henderson's death in 1971, the showroom was only open on Thursdays, for however long the pottery lasted, and still later it opened only on the first Thursday of the month. Collectors would line up at the door at dawn to await opening. The pieces available were few, and the demand was fierce. The Dorchester Pottery Works truly represented a specialized market for people who appreciated fine stoneware of a distinctive design. The closing of the business was sparked by an arson fire, which, in 1979, gutted the pottery works and showroom. In 2001, Bay Cove Human Services acquired the property and renovated the former pottery works for its own use, keeping the kiln room and the kiln itself intact for community exhibitions.

UPHAM'S CORNER MARKET

Upham's Corner has always been a major crossroads, and shoppers had easy access to the commercial district via streetcar lines from Dudley Street, Andrew and Field's Corner stations. This was a thriving area where the Cifrino brothers opened a supermarket at 600–18 Columbia Road; it was known as the first supermarket in this country. The Cifrinos later went on to found the Supreme Market, later to be known as the Purity Supreme Supermarket chain.

Upham's Corner was developed after the Civil War. James Humphreys Upham, who was owner of J.H. Upham & Company, built the Upham Building in 1886 and lived for many years on Jones Hill. His associate was Samuel Bowen Pierce, who lived on Columbia Road. Pierce was born in Vermont in 1804. He entered the crockery business and sold assorted goods throughout New England. After the annexation of Dorchester to Boston in

Upham's Corner Market, the two-story building with awnings on the left, was opened by the Cifrino brothers on Columbia Road in Upham's Corner. The Cifrinos had a market in Boston's North End before they opened what has been called the world's first supermarket in Dorchester.

1870, property values increased, benefiting the Pierce family, which owned large tracts of land. After the death of Samuel B. Pierce, his son demolished his father's house and constructed the building that bears the older man's name, the S.B. Pierce Building. The Columbia Road Automobile Station, managed by Fred Edwards, was built by Pierce's son on the adjacent site. It was here that the proud owners of "horseless carriages" parked their cars and had work done to their new automobiles.

In the 1915, two brothers, John Cifrino (1879–1952) and Paul Cifrino (1891–1945), natives of Salerno, Italy, opened their first store at 786 Dudley Street in Upham's Corner. By 1920, they had Boston architect Willard Bacon design their new store, where they opened the world's first supermarket at 600–18 Columbia Road. William Marnell, author of *Once Upon a Store*, worked for a time at Cifrino's Market in Upham's Corner. Unlike other markets, it stocked a complete line of groceries but did not extend credit or make deliveries and "was the largest general merchandise food market" in Boston. Another thing that made it different was that it was a self-service

John Cifrino (1879–1952) was a native of Salerno, Italy. After the supermarket at Upham's Corner was sold, he became president of Supreme Market on Gallivan Boulevard in Cedar Grove, Dorchester. Eventually, the market merged with a competitor and was known as Purity Supreme Supermarket. *Courtesy of Mary Cifrino Roever.*

store, with clerks only at the checkout counters—the prototype of modern supermarket. Dr. Marnell, who recounts his employment in the store while a student at Harvard, writes, "An amazingly large percentage of a very large and extremely-varied community [shopped] at the store…It was a supermarket in the sense that no supermarket is today. There is nostalgia in memory, but not the kind of nostalgia one might have for the corner grocery store." The Cifrino brothers, who lived nearby on Half Moon Street in Dorchester, ran a well-stocked store that undercut their competitors and included everything from fish to freshly made peanut butter, fresh butter and quality teas and coffee. In his book, Marnell recounts that a woman once asked if the store would sell one egg rather than a dozen. The answer was: "Yes Madam, we sell one egg." Needless to say, the service was prompt and efficient.

The Cifrinos sold the market, which in 1928 had become known as the United Markets, Inc., and in 1934 they opened their new store, Supreme Market, at 540 Gallivan Boulevard in Adams Village. The area of Gallivan Boulevard, or St. Brendan's Parish, was a rapidly growing neighborhood

Paul Cifrino (1891–1945) was a native of Salerno, Italy, and with his elder brother John opened the first supermarket in the world at Upham's Corner. The Cifrinos were astute businessmen who ran a well-stocked store and undercut their competitors. *Courtesy of Mary Cifrino Roever.*

that desperately needed a market. Eventually, Supreme Market was so successful that it merged in 1968 with Purity Markets to become known as the Purity Supreme chain of supermarkets. After World War II, the former Cifrino's Market in Upham's Corner became the Elm Farm Market, still serving the needs of residents but without the quality of service one had come to expect in the past.

Upham's Corner was changing like most city neighborhoods, with many residents buying homes in the suburbs thanks to the automobile and GI loans. Over time, the commercial district changed, and eventually Elm Farm Market closed in the early 1970s. However, thanks to the Dorchester Bay Economic Development Corporation (DBEDC), a nonprofit agency, the Pierce Building was rehabilitated for artist living space in the 1980s, along with the old Cifrino's Market for commercial space and offices. The DBEDC is quoted as saying that it *strive*[s] *to build a strong community by: Developing and preserving modest income homeownership and rental housing; Creating and sustaining commercial and industrial development opportunities and; Building community power through organizing and leadership development.*

HOWARD D. JOHNSON

Howard Johnson created an orange-roofed empire of ice cream shops and restaurants that stretched from Maine to Florida and from the East Coast to the West Coast. Known as the father of the "franchise industry," he revolutionized the restaurant industry in the United States and ensured good food and quality prices that brought customers back for more.

Howard Deering Johnson (1897–1972) was born in Wollaston, a part of Quincy, the son of John H. and Olive Belle Wright Johnson. His father was treasurer of the United Retailers Company, a cigar manufactory on Summer Street in Boston. Howard Johnson left school to begin

Howard Johnson (1897–1972) was the founder of an orange-roofed empire of popular restaurants that stretched from Maine to Florida. He had a hands-on approach to his business and is seen here taste-testing dozens of pies prepared at his kitchens in Quincy to ensure consistent quality before they were distributed to franchise restaurants.

work with his father. He entered World War I, serving in the American Expeditionary Force, Twenty-sixth Infantry Division, in France, and returned after Armistice to work with his father. His father's death in 1921 left him heavily in debt; however, Howard Johnson opened a corner store in 1925 at 93 Beale Street in Quincy, where he had a soda fountain and sold newspapers, cigars and three flavors of ice cream. In the 1920s, Johnson began producing rich ice cream with doubled butterfat and natural ingredients that brought repeat customers; the ice cream was augmented by grilled frankfurters and fried clams. His ice cream stand on Wollaston Beach proved so successful that in 1929 he was able to open his first restaurant in Quincy Square's Granite Trust Building. Here, he opened a restaurant that served New England fare throughout the day, with specials that attracted businesspeople as well as families.

Howard Johnson's restaurant was well placed, located at the junction of Dennis F. Ryan Parkway and Hancock Street in a thriving shopping district. In 1929, Eugene O'Neill's play *Strange Interlude* was banned in Boston by Mayor Malcolm Nichols and the New England Watch & Ward Society and

The Howard Johnson restaurant in Dorchester was opened in 1935 on the Old Colony Parkway (now William T. Morrissey Boulevard) at the foot of Pope's Hill. The parkway was the major highway to and from the city before the Southeast Expressway was built in the mid-1950s, so the restaurant had a prime location and was patronized by hungry travelers.

was moved by the Theatre Guild to Quincy, in a theater opposite Johnson's new restaurant. As the play was extremely long, there was a dinner interlude, and the theatergoers flocked across the street to Howard Johnson's. The restaurant was a great success, but the impact of the Great Depression caused severe problems, and Johnson's bank restricted the credit line his business depended on. The concept of franchising his name was a fairly new business idea, but if he let a franchisee use the Howard Johnson name and purchase all food and supplies from him, he could charge a fee in exchange for the use of his logo, "Simple Simon and the Pie Man." The franchise concept was quite successful, and Johnson is thought of as the father of the modern restaurant franchise in the United States.

Howard Johnson restaurants, in attractive Colonial Revival buildings sporting orange roofs and sea blue shutters, were franchised throughout the New England area. By the late 1930s, with the ascendancy of the automobile, these restaurants were opened on major roads and interstate highways where the traveling public could be assured of consistently high-quality foods that were the same whether served locally or in Maine or Florida. These franchised restaurants sprang up as if by magic throughout the eastern seaboard, serving the same delicious Ipswich clams, grilled frankfurters, chops and steaks and twenty-eight flavors of Johnson's famous ice cream. In 1939, *Reader's Digest* did an article that asked, "Who is Howard Johnson?" His name had become extremely well known through his successful franchise concept. The public had come to expect quality service, affordable prices and family-friendly service, and the restaurants became known as "Landmarks for Hungry Americans."

Opened on June 15, 1935, the restaurant in Dorchester was among the first of the franchises and was awarded to franchisee Harry L. Densberger. Located on the Old Colony Parkway (now known as William T. Morrissey Boulevard) near Neponset Circle, those traveling south in the two decades before the Southeast Expressway was built in the 1950s passed the orange-roofed restaurant, and with ample parking space and a solid tradition of quality and family-friendly service, it was a major attraction for the traveling public. Following World War II, Howard Johnson was expanding so rapidly that his empire was perceived as the world's largest food chain, with hundreds of restaurants serving standardized fare such as fresh roast turkey and the newfangled clam strips, as well as whole clams and twenty-eight flavors of delicious ice cream that the public had come to love. The diligent business acumen was incredible, and Johnson was quoted as saying, "I think that [building my business] was my only form of recreation. I never played golf. I never played tennis. I never did anything after I left school. I ate, slept and thought of nothing but the business."

Howard Johnson retired as president in 1959; his son, Howard Brennan Johnson, assumed his position with a company that had 675 restaurants, 175 motor lodges and annual sales of $127 million. However, the founder never really retired, as he "continued to monitor his restaurants for cleanliness and proper food preparation. He would be chauffeured in a black Cadillac bearing the license plate HJ-28 [his initials and twenty-eight flavors of ice cream] while performing unannounced inspections of the restaurants." He created an orange-roofed empire that attracted the public on a daily basis:

> *His contribution to the restaurant industry was the idea of centralized buying and a commissary system to prepare menu items for distribution to his restaurants. This helped to ensure a uniform consistency and quality, as well as lower costs.*

The American public repaid him in kind, as his name will forever be remembered, along with his restaurants, as the uncontested "King of the Road."

About the Author

Anthony Mitchell Sammarco is a noted historian and author of sixty books on the history and development of Boston, and he lectures widely on the history and development of his native city. He commenced writing in 1995, and his books *Dorchester* and *The Baker Chocolate Company: A Sweet History* have made the bestsellers list. *Boston's Back Bay in the Victorian Era*, *Dorchester: Volume II*, *Dorchester Then & Now*, *Boston's North End* (and *Il North End di Boston* in Italian) and the *Great Boston Fire of 1872*, are among his perennially popular books.

Since 1996, Mr. Sammarco has taught history at the Urban College of Boston, where he was named educator of the year in 2003 and where he serves on the Leadership Council. His course "Boston's Immigrants" was developed especially for the Urban College and its multicultural and diverse student base, and his book *Boston's Immigrants* was written to highlight the diversity of the city and is used in his course. He has received the Bulfinch Award from the Doric Dames of the Massachusetts State House and the Washington Medal from Freedom Foundation and was named Dorchester town historian by Raymond L. Flynn, mayor of Boston, for his work in history. He was elected a fellow of the Massachusetts Historical Society, is a member of the Boston Author's Club and is a proprietor of the Boston Athenaeum. In his volunteer work, he is treasurer of the Victorian Society, New England Chapter, and a trustee of the Forest Hills Cemetery Educational Trust. He is past president of the Bay State Historical League and the Dorchester Historical Society.

He lives in Boston and in Osterville on Cape Cod.

Visit us at

www.historypress.net